Praise For

Stop Shoulding All Over Yourself

Who among us doesn't wrestle with toxic guilt? Who has never been ravaged by unhealthy self-punishment? Who hasn't experienced the damage of unwavering shame? Well, Chris Thurman has done it again! In this eye-opening book, he offers the antidote to self-condemnation, an elixir guaranteed to induce better emotional health, and the secret balm for more grace and compassion - for you and those around you. Don't miss out on this life-changing message.

—Les Parrott, Ph.D.
#1 *New York Times* bestselling author of *Saving Your Marriage Before It Starts*

D1608036

I wish this book had bι
recognized myself in just about every chapter. Chris Thurman's work provides important insight into the struggles that often keep people from recognizing their full God-given potential and, better still, offers a remedy

to put a stop to the "**shoulding**" game. Trust me when I say, you SHOULD buy this book!

—Vicki Courtney
Speaker and bestselling author of *Move On*, *Rest Assured*, and *5 Conversations You Must Have with Your Daughter*, and *5 Conversations You Must Have with Your Son*.

***

"**Should**" is a word we've all said a million times, but Dr. Thurman insightfully helps us see how often it leads to shame, perfectionism, or a critical spirit that we need to let go of so we can become healthier, more loving people. If you want to break free from the shame and self-condemnation caused by "**shoulding**" all over yourself and experience a fuller taste of the abundant life, read this book.

—Pastor John Burke
New York Times bestselling author of *No Perfect People Allowed* and *Imagine Heaven*.

Stop Shoulding All Over Yourself

Making the Journey from
Condemnation to
Compassion

Chris Thurman, Ph.D.

Published by KHARIS PUBLISHING, imprint of
KHARIS MEDIA LLC.

Copyright © 2021 Chris Thurman, Ph.D.

ISBN-13: 978-1-63746-022-1
ISBN-10: 1-63746-022-8

Library of Congress Control Number: 2021934502

All KHARIS PUBLISHING products are available at
special quantity discounts for bulk purchase for sales
promotions, premiums, fund-raising, and educational
needs. For details, contact:

Kharis Media LLC
Tel: 1-479-599-8657
support@kharispublishing.com
www.kharispublishing.com

Let go of who you think you should be in
order to be who you are. Be imperfect
and have compassion for yourself.
--**Brené Brown**

CONTENTS

1   You're Shoulding All Over Yourself   1

2   I Shouldn't Make Mistakes   10

3   I Should Be Able to Get More Done   14

4   I Should Be Able to Control My Circumstances   18

5   I Should Know More Than I Do   22

6   I Should Be Happier Than I Am   26

7   I Shouldn't Do Embarrassing Things   30

8   I Shouldn't Be Addicted to Anything   35

9   I Should Be More Sensitive to Others   39

10   I Shouldn't Forget Things   43

11   I Should Be More Successful   47

12   I Should Like Everything About the Way I Look   52

13   I Should Be Emotionally Smarter   55

14   I Should Be in a Better Mood   60

15   I Should Know What I Want to Do with My Life   64

16   I Shouldn't Have Any Bad Habits   68

17   I Shouldn't Be Losing a Step   72

18   I Shouldn't Have a Bad Bent   76

19   I Should Be a Better Communicator   80

20   I Shouldn't Have Any Unlikeable Qualities   85

21   I Should Have High Self-Esteem   91

22   What Should Have Happened Did   96

Stop Shoulding All Over Yourself Workbook   103

Appendix A: Recommended Reading That Will Help   247
You Stop Shoulding All Over Yourself

Appendix B: References   252

Appendix C: Favorite 'Should' Quotations   253

Chapter 1

You're Shoulding All Over Yourself

Should is a futile word. It's about what didn't happen. It belongs in a parallel universe. It belongs in another dimension of space.
— Margaret Atwood

I was mowing my yard one Saturday in the blistering Texas heat. My yard has a five-foot high brick retaining wall in front of it, so when I mow along that wall, I try to be as careful as possible because I don't want to fall and bring about my own demise.

Unfortunately, on the day in question, I unwisely decided to pirouette on the corner of the retaining wall so I could quickly turn around and mow the next strip of grass. I was about halfway through my pirouette when my foot slipped and I went tumbling down to the sidewalk. Did I mention the retaining wall is five feet high?

For some reason, instead of letting go of the lawnmower, I clamped down on it tighter in my rapid descent to the sidewalk. For five long feet I pressed the handle down as if I had been hit by a taser, and the lawnmower continued to vroom and chug. I almost pulled it on top of me before we both hit the sidewalk with a loud thud and a plume of gas.

Because of my overly strong need for others to think well of me, the first thing I did when I hit the sidewalk was look up and down the street to see if any of my neighbors had been watching. They've seen me do this kind of thing before.

One time, a neighbor saw me with a rope around my waist, hanging outside an upstairs window to clean it and the other upper windows. The other end of the rope was tied to a bedpost inside, although my neighbor did not see that part of my harness. I'm pretty sure my neighbors constantly have their cell phone cameras ready, so they can film me doing something truly idiotic. Fortunately, none of them were outside the day of the lawnmower dance with its dramatic ending.

Once I hit the ground, I must have finally let go of the handle, because the lawnmower was there next to me; if it had been able to speak, it would have said, "You are the biggest idiot on the planet," but it just gave me a shaming look like some of my other tools tend to do. After a few seconds to collect my thoughts, I stood up, sheepishly grabbed the handle of the lawnmower, went back up to the yard, and started mowing again. But that's not all I did, not at all.

No, I spent the rest of the day "shoulding" all over myself about what I had done: *You should have been more careful! You shouldn't walk that close to the edge of the retaining wall! You shouldn't ever pirouette on the corner of your retaining wall like you're a ballerina! You should let someone else mow your grass if you're not going to be more careful! You should have let go of the handle instead of pulling the lawnmower down with you! You shouldn't have…*

Rather than accept what I had done and have compassion for myself for doing it, I took myself out behind the woodshed and gave myself a rousing verbal spanking.

Sadly, I've spent my life "shoulding" all over myself. If you're like me, it's highly likely you've spent your life shoulding all over yourself, as well. Shoulding is usually best friends with "shouldn't-ing," as you'll see.

Shoulding all over ourselves is a common, but unhealthy, way we humans shame and condemn ourselves for being imperfect people, living in an imperfect world, full of other imperfect people. Let me give you some examples:

"I shouldn't have missed my exit," is you shaming and condemning yourself for missing your exit because you weren't paying enough attention (probably because you were on your cell phone) and having to find a place to turn around.

"I should have been on time for the staff meeting," is you shaming and condemning yourself for being late for a staff meeting because you don't always watch the clock carefully enough and sometimes run late to meetings.

"I shouldn't have eaten ten bags of M&Ms," is you shaming and condemning yourself for sometimes mismanaging your emotions in an unhealthy way.

"I shouldn't have yelled at my kids for being so rowdy!" is you shaming and condemning yourself as a parent for occasionally losing your patience with your precious little nose miners when they hang on the ceiling fan and are otherwise out of control (Perhaps, because

3

they ate 10 bags of M&Ms, which you had stashed for yourself).

"I should read more books," is you shaming and condemning yourself because you haven't read a book in ten years and aren't as… how shall I say it?… enlightened a human being as you could be.

"I should move to New Zealand and live the good life," is you shaming and condemning yourself about the painful reality that you do not live in New Zealand, are never, ever going to live in New Zealand, and forever need to more fully accept and embrace where you have lived, do live, and will continue to live.

The flip side of shoulding all over ourselves is that we spend a lot of time shoulding all over others because they're not perfect either. When we should all over others, we're shaming and condemning them for being just as flawed as we are. Let me give you some examples.

"That guy shouldn't be riding my bumper," is you shaming and condemning the guy riding your bumper because he isn't watching what he's doing, is a narcissist who thinks the highway has his name on it or is dealing with an emergency and needs to get around you.

"My waiter should give me better service," is you shaming and condemning your waiter for having a bad hair day because he or she doesn't like being a waiter, thinks customers are overly-demanding jerks, or has some painful situation in their life that is making it hard to focus.

"My friend shouldn't have forgotten my birthday," is you shaming and condemning your friend because you're not the epicenter of his or her universe and they sometimes forget to celebrate special days with you.

"My boss shouldn't be such a royal pain in the butt to work for," is you shaming and condemning your boss for not being very good at managing people and needing to take a year-long class to develop and hone their managerial skills.

"My spouse shouldn't be so hard to live with," is you shaming and condemning your spouse who can be just as selfish and immature as you are regarding how they conduct themselves in the marriage. This reminds me of an old joke: "There are three rings in marriage. The engagement ring, the wedding ring, and suffering." Thank you, please hold your applause, I'll be here all book.

It may sound strange, but the word *should* and its kissing cousin *shouldn't* need to be removed from your vocabulary. There are five important reasons why.

First, emotional health is fundamentally tied to *accepting reality as it is,* rather than stiff-arming it because it isn't the way we would like it to be. When the words, *should* or *shouldn't,* enter our mind and come out of our mouths, that's exactly what we're doing; we're refusing to accept reality, thinking about an ideal world that doesn't exist, and damaging our emotional health in the process.

Second, shoulding all over yourself and others leads to perpetually shaming and condemning everyone in sight for being obviously imperfect human beings. Rather than accept that we *all* fall *far* short of perfection (there's one God, and we ain't it), we become self-destructive, take out the emotional whooping stick, and beat ourselves up unmercifully. You don't need me to tell you this, but that's no way to go through life.

Third, shoulding all over yourself gets in the way of having compassion and empathy for yourself and others. Life is difficult, and, when we should on ourselves and others for being imperfect, we make our lives ten times harder. Having empathy and compassion for yourself and others is the only healthy path toward dealing realistically with human failings, fears, fallacies, and foibles.

Fourth, your shoulds and shouldn'ts reflect your tendency to take something that is *good to want* and turn it into an unhealthy imperative that you demand internally from yourself and externally from others. There is a big difference between "I shouldn't have forgotten my friend's birthday," and "I wish I hadn't forgotten my friend's birthday and will try not to do it again." This may sound like semantics, but it is not. It is critical, even imperative, that you replace your *shoulds* and *shouldn'ts* with *wishes* and *wants* to properly frame your and other people's mistakes, flaws, and miscues.

Fifth, shoulds and shouldn'ts don't lead to constructive change. All the energy you're wasting on shoulding all over yourself and others needs to be channeled in the direction of making healthy changes in your behavior. When you should all over yourself for missing an exit, you're not looking for a place to turn around, all you're doing is driving the wrong direction shoulding on yourself every inch of the way. Shoulding all over yourself is one of the biggest wastes of your time and energy; it neither leads to correcting what you did wrong, nor doing better next time.

I'm not shoulding all over you here about your shoulding all over yourself and others. Far from it. I'm simply telling you that your shoulds and shouldn'ts are a broken part of your psyche; keep you detached from reality; lead you to shame and condemn yourself and others for being human; and you need to do everything you can to break free from them so your life becomes healthier and your relationships with others become more enjoyable.

My goal is to accomplish five important things in this book, but I need your help to do it:

- ❖ First, I'm trying to help you be more consciously aware that you should all over yourself.
- ❖ Second, I'm trying to help you better understand how damaging your shoulds are to your emotional health and your relationships with others.
- ❖ Third, I'm trying to help you more clearly identify the *specific shoulds and shouldn'ts* you have fallen into.
- ❖ Fourth, I'm trying to help you be more compassionate toward yourself and others for thinking this way, given how damaging it is to your life and theirs.
- ❖ Finally, I'm trying to help you channel all that energy you're wasting shoulding all over yourself into making constructive changes so you can live a healthier, more growth-oriented life.

By the end of this book, I hope you will have made the journey from being your own worst enemy to being your own best friend by overcoming your tendency to should all over yourself. As that change happens, you will become a much better friend to others. You'll stop shoulding all over them and you'll have much more compassion and empathy for how difficult and painful life is for all of us during our brief stay on the planet.

In the next twenty chapters (don't worry, they're all short), I walk you through the most destructive shoulds and shouldn'ts we have in life. In each chapter, I use myself as an example of what I'm talking about. I don't do this to make everything about me; I'm the pirouetting lawncare dancer, remember? I use myself as an example because I can speak most clearly and honestly from my own battle with shoulding all over myself. I'm happy to share my experiences in the hope they will encourage you to live a should-free life.

Some final thoughts about how to read this book before I close this chapter:

First, I *strongly suggest* after you read each chapter, go to the *Stop Shoulding on Yourself Workbook* in the back and complete the corresponding lesson. I want you to *learn* a lot of things from reading this book, but I want you to make sure you *apply* what you learn so you can grow into a healthier, more loving human being. *Please, take doing the lessons in the workbook just as seriously as you take reading the chapters.* You'll get so much more out of this book if you do.

Second, I wrote this book so it could be used individually or in groups, but I want to encourage you to go through it with others. When we're trying to face our issues, there is something about joining with others that makes that task richer and more fulfilling. I hope you will get a group of people together to explore the concepts in this book and challenge each other to apply them.

Third, you are not going to identify with every should or shouldn't I explore. As you read the book, try to figure out which shoulds and shouldn'ts are harming your emotional health and relationships the most. By the end of the book, I hope you will have figured out your two to three shoulds or shouldn'ts that are the biggest barriers to having the life you were meant to have.

Fourth, I want you to try to have compassion and empathy for yourself and others as you read the book. Life is difficult, we are flawed, and the combination of the two makes everyone's life painful. Try to have compassion for the fact we are all in this together and need to encourage and support each other along the way.

See you in the next chapter. Oh, don't forget to do the lesson in the *Stop Shoulding All Over Yourself Workbook* first.

Chapter 2

I Shouldn't Make Mistakes

To err is human, but when the eraser wears out
ahead of the pencil, you're overdoing it.
—Josh Jenkins

When I was in college, I worked every summer to make as much money as possible to pay for school. One summer, I worked for a construction supply company. One of the things this supply company sold was sliding glass doors.

My work compadres and I would put these sliding glass doors together in the warehouse before we delivered them to customers. But these weren't just any sliding glass doors; they were double-insulated sliding glass doors that were pretty heavy and fairly expensive.

One day, mostly out of boredom, I noticed things were getting dirty underneath the crate containing all these double-insulated glass panels, so I got the bright idea to hop on the forklift, raise the crate, and sweep everything out from underneath. I am a compulsive neat freak. It was *really* bothering me that these danged, heavy, pricey double-insulated glass panels were in a crate that had dirt underneath it. The crate was fine about it, not a problem. I was bothered and not fine about it.

Hindsight says I probably didn't put very much thought into all this, which is not unusual for me when

I'm on a mission to clean things up. No sooner had I lifted this big, honking crate a couple of feet off the ground, then all the danged double-glass panels titled forward, flew out of the crate like clowns shot out of a circus cannon, and down they came crashing to the ground.

My boss came flying out of his office to see what all the ruckus was about and saw the three million pieces of safety glass on the floor of his warehouse mixed with all the dirt that had been under the crate to begin with.

My boss was a good guy. Even though I had just cost him thousands of dollars, he didn't jump my case or make a big deal out of what I had done. I think he saw that I was trying to do something good by cleaning up the warehouse. Unfortunately, he didn't need to get on me about it because I was more than happy to do that myself.

For the next week or so, I did nothing but beat myself up for making that mistake. I felt like I should offer my boss the remainder of my summer pay to reimburse him for all the glass panels I broke. All he wanted me to do was clean up the mess and be more careful. All I wanted to do was take myself out behind the warehouse woodshed and beat myself up for being such a stupid idiot and messing everything up.

Please notice that in this situation I was beating myself up for making a mistake that was *amoral;* it had nothing to do with acting *immorally.* If you're like me, you beat yourself up *even more* when you do something immoral in life. As strange as this may sound, I don't want you shaming and condemning yourself, even when you act immorally. Why? Because even beating yourself

11

up for acting immorally drains away the energy you need to correct what you did and to work harder on not doing it again. Whether your mistakes in life are *amoral or immoral*, don't beat yourself up for making them. Doing that only makes it harder for you to grow into a healthier, more moral person.

How about you? Do you allow yourself to be a human being who makes mistakes without beating yourself up about them? Or, do you react to your mistakes with great alarm, shock, and self-condemnation?

I want to challenge all of us to more-fully accept and be more compassionate that we humans are mistake machines BUT condemning ourselves about it has to stop. I want all of us, especially when we are trying to do something helpful or constructive, to get off our own backs about being mistake-prone.

My unhealthy mantra over the years has been, "To err is human, but to really screw things up takes someone like me!" That's just gotta stop. We all need to embrace the fact that to err is human and leave it at that. If we beat ourselves up for making mistakes, we are stiff-arming one of the most important truths of all: It is human nature to make a mistake and mess things up in the process.

I'm not arguing for human sloppiness here. If all you do is make one mistake after another, with no effort to correct, you're not working hard enough toward growing and improving as a human being. The quote at the start of this chapter is right—if your eraser wears out ahead of your pencil, you're overdoing being a mistake-prone human being.

So, the next time you make a mistake or do something wrong, please don't beat yourself up about it. We can't do anything perfectly. Not even close. Allow being imperfect to be okay while you're still trying to do the best you can.

I'm thankful I had a boss who didn't put me down because I was human and made a mistake. I'm thankful he gave me grace and forgave what I did. And I'm going to keep trying to internalize his view that "to err is human," so when I make my next mistake, I simply smile, clean up the mess, and learn from what I did.

We would all be wise to follow the advice of author Les Brown, "Give yourself a break. Stop beating yourself up! Everyone makes mistakes, has setbacks and failures. You don't come with a book on how to get it right all the time. You will fail sometimes, not because you planned to, but simply because you're human. Failure is a part of creating a great life. Stand up to it and handle it with grace."

Chapter 3

I Should Be Able to Get More Done

If you want your life to have impact, focus it!
Stop dabbling. Stop trying to do it all. Do less.
Prune away even good activities and do only
that which matters most. Never confuse activity
with productivity. You can be busy without
a purpose, but what's the point?
--Rick Warren

I wrote my doctoral dissertation on Type A behavior. Type A's are driven, impatient, competitive, easily-irritated, hyper-productivity-oriented people who can develop heart disease separate and apart from having any other risk factors. Type A's have a bad case of what they call "hurry sickness," and the reason I chose to do my dissertation on Type A behavior is because I'm Type A.

The hyper-productivity part of being Type A is my toughest battle. Type A's are prone to trying to multi-task and get as much done as possible in the shortest amount of time possible. Because we are that way, we rarely feel we get enough done, even though we often get more done than others in the same amount of time.

Let me give you a personal example. In the last ten years or so, I've gotten into landscaping my yard. When Holly and I bought our "empty nest" home years ago, the front yard was a disaster, something that had me licking my lips in anticipation of making my yard look like the Garden of Eden. I'm not exaggerating here. When we bought the house, the front yard was nothing but pea gravel and dead bushes. It's the main reason I bought the house—so I could take it from being an eyesore and turn it into something beautiful.

I couldn't wait to start working on my yard. Unfortunately, the yard was a tad resistant to me working on it. The dead bushes must have had root systems that went down five hundred feet; there were three or four trees I had to remove; and given how deep it was, the previous owner must have paid someone to put thirteen tons of pea gravel in the yard.

Not being one to ever pay anybody to do work for me (I say I'm frugal, others say I'm cheap), I was determined to do the yard myself. That was my first mistake. I honestly don't know how many hours I've spent getting my yard to look like the Garden of Eden, but it is no exaggeration to say it must be in the hundreds. Easily.

The point is, I didn't cut myself much slack when I went out into the yard to get things done. I began every Saturday thinking I was going to get a lot of things accomplished, only to run into how much time and energy things really took and problems coming up that I didn't anticipate.

One Saturday, I spent over an hour just trying to pull out *one bush* that had a particularly nasty set of roots. I didn't go into the yard that day planning to spend an hour on one bush. I was foolish enough to think I would merely grab the bush by what was sticking out of the ground, give it a good yank, and it would come flying out of mother earth, straight into my wheelbar-row. Silly me!

After it took an hour to get as much of the bush out as possible, I was exhausted and in no mood to finish the rest of my day in the yard. Nevertheless, I perse-vered. I turned my attention to the bush's brother that was planted right next to it. Same thing. It took me an hour to remove it. I grew even more Type A-ish about this unfolding drama, angrier, more impatient, and less and less satisfied with how much I was getting done.

As I labored over multiple Saturdays to remove all the dead bushes and pea gravel, I put in new bushes and tried to get sod to grow in the yard. I must not have a bona fide green thumb, because pretty much everything I planted died. As a result, I re-planted bushes and sod over and over. To this day, my family makes fun of how often I've replanted the yard in my efforts to create earthly perfection.

I wish you could see my yard today. It's a work of art. I would put my yard on par with the gardens at the Palace of Versailles (when I visited there, I saw a few problems with how they were doing things that I would have been happy to correct for them). All this is *nine years* after I began my initial quest to conquer the eyesore my yard used to be and turn it into something awesome. I can already tell some plants aren't going to make it through this winter, so I'm eagerly looking for-ward to pulling them up next spring and trying some-thing new.

The bottom line here is, you're a human being who can only be in one place at a time, doing the best you can do, to get as much done as one human being can do. Don't should all over yourself when your efforts don't seem to produce much. You got done what you got done. I want you to give yourself an "attaboy" or "attagirl" for all you accomplished.

One of my favorite quotes is from Richard Monckton Milnes, "The virtue lies in the struggle, not the prize." That's the attitude we driven, hyper-productivity-oriented Type A's need to have. At the end of the day, the victory doesn't lie in how much we got done, but in the fact we really worked hard at it. We need to pat ourselves on the back for that.

I close this chapter with another one of my favorite quotes when it comes to our efforts to get things done. Franklin Roosevelt said, "It is not the critic who counts; not the man who points out how the strong man stumbles, or where the doer of deeds could have done them better. The credit belongs to the man who is actually in the arena, whose face is marred by dust and sweat and blood; who strives valiantly;… who at best knows in the end the triumph of high achievement, and who at worst, if he fails, at least fails while daring greatly."

For those of us who are Type A's and never feel like we get nearly enough done, I want us to memorize and meditate on Roosevelt's important statement each and every day. I put a lot of sweat and blood into transforming my yard into something beautiful, and I sure didn't need to criticize myself along the way for what wasn't getting done. My effort was my victory. If we persevere at things over time, we ultimately accomplish quite a bit. Don't should all over yourself about how much or how little you're getting done, just pat yourself on the back because you gave it your best shot.

Chapter 4

I Should Be Able to Control My Circumstances

I was kind of surprised to learn how controlling I am. I never thought of myself in that way. I think the root of the control issues is usually fear, because you want to know what's going to be happening at any given moment.
—Michelle Pfeiffer

Have you ever been called a control freak? I have, and justifiably so. I've spent way too much of my life trying to control things *outside of me* (people, circumstances, opportunities, bad situations) rather than working on controlling the things *inside of me* (thoughts, feelings, and actions).

Here's an example of what I'm talking about: I don't like to drive. Why? Because for some unknown reason, other motorists won't let me control their driving behavior. They won't let me make them use their turn indicators, go faster in the fast lane, go slower in the slow lane, get off my bumper, not run red lights, yield to me when I'm trying to merge into traffic, get off their cell phones while driving, pay more attention, slow down in the fast lane, go faster in the slow lane, make a right turn at a red light after coming to a complete stop, come to a complete stop at Stop signs, slow down in parking lots, speed up in parking lots, use one parking spot for their car instead of two, not park so close to my car in a parking lot, not ding my car with their car door, and five hundred other things they won't let me control.

Did I tell you I don't like to drive? Hard to imagine, isn't it!

So, what's the problem? Well, as you can tell from everything I said, the problem is that people don't give two hoots about how I think they should drive and aren't going to let me control their driving behavior. I don't understand that, but that's just the way it is.

If you're not careful, you can should all over yourself that you aren't powerful enough to control the world and everything going on in it. You can end up becoming bitter and resentful that others don't care what you think and are going to drive the way they want to drive, eat the way they want to eat, worship the way they want to worship, love whom they want to love, work the way they want to work, party the way they want to party, and spend money the way they want to spend money. And it is especially maddening when they happily tell you to buzz off if you don't like it.

When I think about the issue of control, I'm drawn to Reinhold Niebuhr's *Serenity Prayer*, "*God grant me the serenity to accept the things I cannot change; courage to change the things I can; and wisdom to know the difference. Living one day at a time; enjoying one moment at a time; accepting hardships as the pathway to peace; taking, as He did, this sinful world as it is, not as I would have it; trusting that He will make all things right if I surrender to His Will; that I may be reasonably happy in this life and supremely happy with Him forever in the next. Amen.*"[1] If you're like me, you've spent too much time refusing to accept that there are things in life you cannot change because they are not under your control.

I don't say any of this to put us down; that would be completely inappropriate in a book trying to get you to stop shoulding all over yourself and have more compassion about the fact that life is painful and difficult. I say all this just to gently remind us that a well-lived life is one in which we stop trying to control the things we can't and keep trying to exercise greater control over ourselves.

I suggest we switch from trying to *control* others to trying to *influence* them. The best way to influence others is to practice what we preach. If I want to influence a friend to treat me better, I need to treat them well. If I wanted to influence my kids to have good table manners growing up, I needed to have good manners when I was eating with them. If I want to influence you to stop shoulding all over yourself, I need to model that for you by not shoulding on myself when I make mistakes or should on you when you make them.

May I also suggest that we switch from trying to control others to having greater self-control? Each day, we think all kinds of things, have all kinds of emotions, and exhibit all kinds of actions. If control is your thing, keep trying to bring your thoughts, feelings, and actions under greater self-control, so the next time someone

[1] Niebuhr, R.
https://prayerfoundation.org/dailyoffice/serenity_prayer_full_version.htm

rides your bumper or cuts in front of you in life, you handle it like a mature adult.

Don't should all over yourself when you can't control others. The painful truth of the matter is you can't. Everybody's got free will, and they don't appreciate it when you're trying to control how they express it. Keep trying to influence others (by practicing what you preach) while working on greater self-control over how you think, what you feel, and how you act.

And, please don't should all over yourself when you struggle to control yourself. Self-control is a tough nut to crack. Instead, I encourage you to be compassionate toward yourself as you try to exercise greater control over your thoughts, feelings, and actions, while also trying to resist the urge to control the thoughts, feelings, and actions of others. It's a worthy aspiration to have in life, but a really tough mountain to climb.

Control others? Not a good strategy. Influence others by practicing what you preach? A wonderful thing. Develop greater self-control? Fantastic!

An update on my controlling attitude about driving: While I'm not there yet, it's a lot better. Since I started working on controlling *my thoughts, feelings, and actions* toward my fellow motorists, rather than trying to control their driving behavior, I've been much more at peace about how people drive. And, it's been a while since I gave anybody a dirty look or thought about running them off the road. I feel pretty good about that.

It's amazing how much we can enjoy life when we stop trying to control what's going on outside of us and work on trying to control what's going on inside of us. Try it, you'll like it.

Chapter 5

I Should Know More Than I Do

*Education is learning what you didn't
even know you didn't know.*
—**Daniel J. Boorstein**

I was walking across campus one day at the University of Texas when an unusual thought entered my mind. I was a graduate student at the time, headed to the library to do some research on my doctoral dissertation. It hit me that the University of Texas, like most institutions of higher education, has dozens and dozens of academic areas in which they grant doctorates, most of which I knew nothing about.

My alma mater grants doctorates in engineering, accounting, physics, architecture, finance, marketing, advertising, special education, art history, music, geological sciences, American studies, anthropology, comparative literature, economics, French, Latin American studies, philosophy, religious studies, sociology, biochemistry, computer science, human development, nursing, pharmaceutical science, public policy, and my area, psychology, just to name a bunch. Except for psychology, I didn't know diddly about all those areas of study in which the University of Texas granted *doctorates*.

As I continued my trek to the library, it hit me that I had chosen to get my doctorate in psychology, but within the field of psychology there are numerous doctoral programs. You can get a doctoral degree in experimental psychology, developmental psychology, child psychology, organizational psychology, social psychology, cognitive psychology, evolutionary psychology, forensic psychology, school psychology, sports psychology, health psychology, educational psychology, clinical psychology, and my area, counseling psychology, just to name a bunch. With the exception of counseling psychology, I didn't know diddly about all those areas of psychology with doctoral programs, and I have a doctorate in psychology.

As I kept walking, it hit me that within the field of counseling psychology there were a zillion things one could learn, from all the various mental disorders, counseling theories and techniques, to research methods for studying human behavior. I have a PhD in counseling psychology, and to this day, I still don't know very much about all the different areas of study that fall within the field of counseling psychology.

Finally, it hit me that I was doing my doctoral dissertation on Type A behavior and that there were numerous areas within Type A behavior one could study. As I mentioned earlier, Type A's are coronary attack-prone people who are driven, hard-working, success-oriented, impatient, competitive, work obsessed, aggressive, easily angered folks (basically, I studied myself). You could do numerous dissertations on any of those specific areas. I studied the relationship between irrational beliefs and Type A behavior, and to this day, I still don't know diddly about all those other aspects of being Type A. Did I say I did my doctoral dissertation on Type A behavior?

So, let me land the airplane here and tell you what I'm trying to tell you. Another way we should all over ourselves as human beings is that we get down about the fact we don't know very much while we're here. But, as you can see from my long-winded pontifications above, it is an inescapable part of being human, because what can be known is much too vast.

Let me put this a little differently. If all that could be known adds up to 100%, on our best day, we don't know but 0.00001% of all that, and I'm being generous. That applies to Nobel Prize winning laureates, as well. As much as they know, compared to us mere mortals, they don't know diddly compared to what can be known. Humble Nobel laureates will tell you that.

If that didn't get through to you, let me say it another way. Google estimates that there are over one hundred and thirty million books in existence. That's million with an "m." Of all the books currently available to read, I would guess that most of us haven't read any more than 0.00001% of those books. Again, I think I'm being generous.

In case you think my numbers are off about the percentage of books we are likely to have read before we kick the bucket, .00001% of 130,000,000 is 1,300. See, I was giving us credit for reading 1,300 books during our lifetimes and was actually thinking pretty highly of us! The average person doesn't read 1,300 books; researchers suggest that Americans, on average, read 12 books a year. That sounds a tad high to me, but let's assume it is true. The average female lives to be 81, so she will read about 972 books in a lifetime. The average male will live to be 76, so he will read about 912 books in a lifetime.

I'm not equating reading a book to knowledge acquisition here; I'm simply trying to make the point that, given our reading habits, *we are not going to know very much* compared to what *can be known* as we live out our lives. And, given that women read, on average, 60 more books in their lifetimes than men, I'm also trying to make the point that women end up knowing a lot more than men. (Please, men, go pick up this book from across the room where you just threw it.)

Far too often, we put ourselves down because we know only the tiniest fraction of all that can be known. Far too often, we say, "I didn't know that," as if it's a surprise or insult, rather than a humble acknowledgement, as we walk across the campus of life, of how immense what can be known happens to be.

We would all be wise to accept what Copernicus, one of the most knowledgeable people of his day, said over five-hundred years ago, "To know that we know what we know, and to know that we do not know what we do not know, that is true knowledge." That's someone who knows quite a bit, compared to us mere mortals.

The next time you're down on yourself for how little you know and the mistakes that flow out of not knowing very much, please take a deep breath; let it be okay that you, like the rest of us, don't know diddly, compared to what can be known. Stop beating yourself up about it. Have some compassion for yourself and others that it's true. Along the way in life, simply learn as much as you can and do the best you can to properly apply what you know.

Chapter 6

I Should Be Happier Than I Am

Even a happy life cannot be without a measure of darkness, and the word happy would lose its meaning if it were not balanced by sadness. It is far better to take things as they come along with patience and equanimity.
—**Carl Jung**

Happiness is a little overrated, don't you think? If all we ever felt was happy, wouldn't it be rather boring? If all we ever felt was happy, how would we know that we were happy? We'd have nothing else to compare it to. Yeah, happiness is over-rated.

This chapter is my effort to challenge you not to should all over yourself that you're not happy all the time, and to have compassion about it for yourself. Wanting to be happy all the time is unhealthy, because there are a lot of things to be unhappy about in life. Besides, attaching your happiness to the wrong things is unhealthy because you're only going to get your heart broken when those things let you down.

That being said, it's not a bad thing to want to be reasonably happy, especially at the right time and for the right reasons. I say "at the right time and for the right reasons" because we often pursue happiness at the wrong time and in the wrong way. A personal example might help.

I've put a lot of my happiness into whether or not people like me. Yep, I'm an approval junkie. There's nothing wrong with wanting others to like us; that's only human. The problem arises when we make being liked and accepted too important, then feel crushed when others don't think we're the best chili at the cook-off.

My unhealthy need to be liked never made it okay that some people didn't like me. I can't begin to tell you how emotionally painful it has been to not be liked by *everyone*, and why I've been working my whole life to stop needing *everyone's* approval.

All this reminds me of when I was in graduate school. As a doctoral student, I was fortunate to land a gig as an instructor in the educational psychology department and teach an undergraduate class on coping with stress and anxiety, something I enjoyed to no end. Every day in the classroom was pure joy to me.

The only problem was that the students evaluated their instructors and professors at the end of each semester and got to do it anonymously. To make matters worse, the department administrators didn't send you the evaluations until a couple of months after the class ended. I'm sure the University of Texas didn't want to risk lawsuits because instructors and professors were tracking students down who had given them negative evaluations. Given my overly strong need for approval, I dreaded receiving the class evaluations in the campus mail, being so sure that I was going to get lambasted.

I'll never forget one semester as long as I live. I got the evaluations in the middle of the summer after teaching a class in the spring. One evaluation after another was positive, and my spirit soared... until I read one student's evaluation. Apparently, he didn't think I was the best thing since sliced bread and wrote the following statement in the Comments section: "This was not UT's finest moment." That crushed me.

I got thirty-five evaluations that day, all but one of them positive. Did I allow myself to be happy about that? Of course not. I spent the rest of that summer and fall thinking about that one disgruntled student. I secretly hoped I could figure out who he was, find him, and give him a piece of my mind. But, that's why student evaluations are anonymous and sent to you after you've handed out grades.

My tendency to put my happiness in the hands of whether or not others like me has been a very unhealthy thing. Rather than put my happiness in the hands of doing things I enjoy and find meaningful, I've spent my life putting it in the hands of whether or not people like or accept me. Not a good decision.

How about you? Have you tied your happiness to things like people's approval, how much you achieve, how much money you make, climbing the corporate ladder, having expensive possessions, how you look, or things going your way? Or have you tied your happiness to doing the things that light your fire in life and give you a sense of meaning and purpose?

If we put our happiness in the hands of things we can't control, we are inviting a lot of unhappiness to come our way. Even when we don't, we are going to feel happy at times about how things are going, and unhappy at times, as well. Happiness is tied to happenstance, so its fluctuation is inevitable in life. Stop shoulding all over yourself because there are times you experience the normal (inevitable) unhappiness of being a human being in a fallen world.

"This was not UT's finest moment." To whoever wrote that, I'm genuinely sorry you didn't like the class, but I want you to know I enjoyed teaching you and was happy the whole time I was doing it.

Chapter 7

I Shouldn't Do Embarrassing Things

Every day, I have a most embarrassing moment.
—Steven Hill

I know it's not a good thing, but I enjoy watching "Most Embarrassing Fails" videos on YouTube™. It never ceases to amaze me that we humans have such a remarkable ability to do really stupid things and humiliate ourselves in the process.

I watched a few embarrassing fails videos recently and just had to shake my head at how creative we can be when it comes to doing some wild and crazy things that result in quite painful and embarrassing consequences.

I watched people fall down flights of stairs, walk into glass doors, fall into ponds while trying to walk on ice, follow their bowling ball down the lane only to fall on their rumps, and do karate kicks that hit innocent bystanders in the face.

I watched people cut the tree limbs they were standing on, fall off a stage, pole dance and spin out of control, tow a car only to pull the front fender off, and ride a motorcycle *inside their home,* only to crash it into a wall.

Some folks tried to hit golf balls from inside their homes, only to break their sliding glass doors, execute skateboard tricks that had painful encounters with the laws of physics, dance on a table, break it and come crashing to the floor, try to jump over steel and concrete posts, only to rack themselves, and fall into a pool while taking a selfie. And don't get me started on how *our* epic fails often come crashing down on our kids. It's fortunate that children are made out of rubber, otherwise, Child Protective Services would have to be on speed dial.

I'm bringing all this up because another thing I don't want you shoulding all over yourself about is the fact that you do embarrassing things. Once again: You do embarrassing things. We all do. It's part of being human, although admittedly sometimes an injurious and humiliating part. Let me share a personal example.

After I got my doctorate, my first position was a joint appointment as an assistant professor in psychology and counselor in the student counseling center at the University of North Texas. Holly and I moved to Denton (about 40 miles northeast of Dallas) and began our new adventure. A couple of years later, we had our first kiddo, Matt. Shortly after Matt was born, Holly asked me if I would mind watching him while she went on a jog around our apartment complex.

A few minutes after she left, I got the bright idea of sticking one of Matt's toys on my forehead and stepping out on the deck of our apartment to see if Holly noticed me as she jogged by. The toy was a small ball with little balls inside of it that was attached to a suction cup. I stuck this thing to my forehead, thinking to myself it felt pretty dang tight, and stepped out on the deck.

Five minutes later, after watching car after car go by with occupants wondering if I had lost my mind, Holly

31

came whipping around the apartment complex. She looked up, saw what I'd done, and gave me that look that said, "I wish I'd never married you; I could have done so much better." Apparently, she didn't find me as charming and funny as I found myself. So, I went back into the apartment, took the dang thing off my forehead, plopped down on the floor, and began watching college football.

About thirty minutes later, Holly came into the apartment and her eyes got bigger than silver dollars. She said, "You'd better go look in the mirror." I replied, "What?" She replied, "You'd just better go look in the mirror."

Following her advice, I stepped into the bathroom, only to see a huge, dark purple hickey on my forehead. Apparently, the suction cup on the toy was a pretty good one. My first thought was, "You idiot—only you would give yourself a hickey on your forehead!" I soon discovered that there wasn't a make-up base on the planet that could cover that unsightly, self-inflicted, forehead hickey.

The main thought I had was, *Here I am, a professor and counselor at a university, and I'm going to be walking around campus with a huge, dark purple hickey on my forehead next week.* It didn't go away quickly, either; I had to walk around with that thing on my forehead for a couple of weeks.

My graduate students would ask me, "Dr. Thurman, how'd you get that hickey on your forehead?" Not that I was defensive about it, but I would reply, "Well, if you must know, I stuck my kid's toy on my forehead!" They would give me that "I don't believe you" look, as if I were part of a satanic cult or into some unusual personal practices when I was off campus.

I say all this to let you know that we are all human; we sometimes do things that, upon further review, we know were pretty embarrassing and wish we hadn't done. I think that's why I like watching embarrassing fails videos on YouTube™. Misery loves company, and I find some degree of (sick) pleasure in knowing other people can be as stupid as I am. I agree with Albert Einstein on this, "Only two things are infinite, the universe and human stupidity, and I'm not sure about the former."

I'm thankful that cell phones weren't around when I stuck Matt's toy on my forehead. I'm thankful because there is no video evidence of what I did, so if anyone from my past were to bring this up, I would categorically deny it happened. I feel for all the people whose epic fails were recorded for posterity and uploaded to YouTube™. That's gotta hurt even more than the failure itself, plus knowing millions can watch them over and over and over.

As you go through life, don't should all over yourself that you are going to do some of the stupidest, most embarrassing things imaginable. Have compassion for yourself about it. The next time you fall down a flight of stairs, follow your bowling ball down the lane, walk into a glass door, cut off a tree limb you're standing on, fall into a pool while taking a selfie, break through the ice while walking on a frozen pond, rack yourself trying to jump over a fence post, or stick your kid's toy to your forehead and give yourself a hickey, be kind. Don't you think the pain and embarrassment were enough punishment? Just be glad no one videoed it. At least for your sake, I hope no one did.

Chapter 8

I Shouldn't Be Addicted to Anything

*To be alive is to be addicted, and to be alive and
addicted is to stand in need of grace.*
—**Gerald May**

Everyone has addictions. You may not agree, but it's true. Everyone on the planet is addicted, and we are not just addicted to one or two things, but to many things.

Using the term somewhat loosely, I believe you can be addicted to alcohol, opioids, food, gambling, gaming, the internet, texting, caffeine, nicotine, sex, shopping, work, marijuana, exercise, television, approval, yardwork, neatness, punctuality, being late, romance novels, being right, crossword puzzles, being hard-headed, running from your issues, avoiding responsibility, lying, being lazy, collecting Precious Moments figurines, falling in love, being competitive, anger, sadness, anxiety, chaos, being a jerk, blaming others, cross-stitching, being cheap, giving too much, rescuing people from their bad choices, looking in the mirror, being vain, not really listening to others, driving too fast, and working out, just to name a few dozen.

I've spent my life being addicted to many things, one of which I'm willing to tell you about: Sports. As far back as I can remember, I've loved playing sports, but I unhealthily allowed it to morph into an addiction. Growing up, I played baseball before becoming a tennis player. I could never play enough of those two sports and would go through a form of withdrawal when I couldn't play. Later, I took up racquetball and couldn't play enough racquetball to satisfy my craving to play that sport. After that, I took up golf, and, you guessed it, I found myself playing way too much golf and being unhappy when something got in the way of getting to play.

I want to focus on my addiction to golf for a minute. I played a little bit of golf when I was a kid but was too addicted to baseball and tennis to pay much attention to it. It was years later when my son Matt started playing golf that I took it up again. And, boy, did I get hooked in a hurry. I immediately started playing every chance I got and played as many holes as I could when I was out on a golf course.

One particular moment in my addiction to golf comes to mind. I started playing very early one morning and stopped playing only after the sun went down, and that was just because I couldn't see where my ball was landing anymore. Any guess as to how many holes I played that day? Fifty-seven. Keep in mind that I walked, carried my own bag, and that it was summer in Texas.

You have to be pretty addicted to golf to play that many holes in one day, especially in the Texas heat. When I got home, I had a lot of splaining to do about why I stayed out there that long, and finally it dawned on me that I had taken something good and enjoyable in life and let it become an addiction.

I'm happy to report that after a number of years of working on my addiction to golf, it is finally in a much better place. I've gone from playing way too much to playing a reasonable amount, such that when I play now I actually look forward to it, rather than feel like I'm taking another joyless hit like the most addicted drug addict on the planet. I never thought it would happen, but I've probably played, on average, a couple rounds of golf a month over the last few years. My golf buddies are none too happy with me, but they understand that I had let golf become way too important; they are graciously willing to support my efforts to step away and put golf in its proper place in my life.

I feel some degree of shame that I took a sport and allowed it to become an addiction. I feel some shame that I put golf ahead of my family and living a life of greater balance. I feel shame that I was so addicted to golf that I would play fifty-seven holes in one day while carrying my own golf bag in the Texas heat, something I used to boast about. I'm just thankful that those days are behind me, that I've gotten "sober," and that when I do play it is enjoyable and fun.

I could have gone into a bunch of other things in talking about my addictions. I've been addicted to work, music, approval, Blue Bell™ ice cream (Cookies 'n Cream and Chocolate Chip are my two personal favorites), following Texas Longhorn football, perfection, cleanliness, television, YouTube™ videos, yardwork, being agreed with, doing seminars, keeping people at arm's length, isolating, ruminating about past hurts, being angry and sad . . . I think you get the point.

How about you? What addictions do you have? Whatever you do, don't should all over yourself for being an addict. Everyone is. Have compassion that your life has been damaged by these addictions; be kind to yourself as you embark on an effort to break free from them. The last thing we addicts need is more self-condemnation. The first thing we need is grace. Give yourself some grace and keep putting one foot in front of the other in your journey to live as free from addictions as you can. As French psychologist Emile Coue put it, "Day by day, in every way, I am getting better and better."

Chapter 9

I Should Be More Sensitive to Others

*It is, for example, axiomatic that we should
all think of ourselves as being more sensitive
than other people because, when we are
insensitive in our dealings with others, we
cannot be aware of it at the time: conscious
insensitivity is a self-contradiction.*
—**W. H. Auden**

Yes, I'm suggesting there are times when you are insensitive to others and don't even realize it. That's true of all of us. I just don't want you to should all over yourself about it.

If your initial reaction to the title of this chapter was, "I'm very sensitive!" you're probably talking about the fact that you're an *overly* sensitive person when it comes to reacting to the things people do that wound you. I'm not talking about that version of sensitivity. I'm talking about not being sensitive to how your actions wound others and not having enough empathy for how they feel about it.

To drive this home, I want to share with you how insensitive I was to my family because of my addiction to work. For years, I was in denial about how often I put work ahead of them, justifying it by patting myself on the back that I was providing for my family and making sure they had every opportunity in life to spread their wings.

What a load of nonsense. I wasn't a workaholic for them, I was a workaholic for myself. Work was how I tried to assuage feeling I was a loser. Sure, working hard was a way I made sure I put enough bacon on the table for my family to be properly taken care of, but, if I'm totally honest, it was mostly for me.

The worst example of this, and it haunts me to this day, is when I was traveling to another city each week to do personal growth seminars. I did that for several years, leaving Holly and the kids behind to fend for themselves. It pains me to say it, but one time I did 120 day-long seminars in one year (I averaged 2.3 full-day seminars a week that year). Given that I would always leave on a Sunday and come back on a Wednesday, I was away from home 160 days that year. That means I was home only 56% of the time.

At the time, I didn't think much about how all this was affecting Holly and the kids. I didn't spend time thinking about what it was like for Holly to have all the responsibility of the kids on her shoulders and be without the love and support of her husband because he was gone. I didn't think about what it was like for my young children to not have their dad around enough to help them with homework, read bedtime stories, or play catch in the yard.

I only compounded the problem by returning home from my weekly professional jaunts and immediately going into catch-up mode with all the things I had put on hold in my private practice and around the house while I was gone. I wasn't all that much more available to my family when I was home than when I was away because I've always put work ahead of relationships.

Harry Chapin's song, *Cat's in the Cradle*©, was something I more than identified with as my kids got older and left home. These lines always make my stomach hurt:

> *My son turned ten just the other day*
> *He said "Thanks for the ball, Dad, come on let's play*
> *Can you teach me to throw," I said "Not today*
> *I got a lot to do," he said "That's okay"*
> *And he walked away but his smile never dimmed*
> *And said, "I'm gonna be like him, yeah*
> *You know I'm gonna be like him."*[2]

You don't realize at the time that you are being insensitive to those you love. Awareness that you're being insensitive typically comes *after* the fact, when you can't go back in time and undo the past. Nevertheless, if we care about having been hurtful and insensitive to those we love, we make amends in the here-and-now to let them know we're truly sorry and don't want to hurt them anymore.

Once I started walking around in my family's shoes and feeling their pain about what it was like to have me for a spouse and a dad, I began to come to my senses. I finally began to be more sensitive to their feelings, how painful my absences had been, and how I needed to

---

[2] Harry Chapin, *Cat's in the Cradle*,
https://www.azlyrics.com/lyrics/harrychapin/catsinthecradle.html

invest so much more in their lives to make our home healthier.

I am blessed to have a very gracious and forgiving family. They have been patient about me overcoming my workaholism and trying to engage with them more deeply. I will never be able to thank them enough for being that way, given how many years I was insensitive to all the ways my actions were negatively impacting their lives.

Don't should all over yourself that you have been insensitive and hurtful to those you love. Open up your heart, turn on your ears, and dedicate yourself to being more engaged with those you love. Everyone's life will get so much better.

Chapter 10

I Shouldn't Forget Things

*As you get older three things happen. The
first is your memory goes, and I can't
remember the other two.*
—Norman Wisdom

Since forgetting things is only going to get worse as
we get older, we might as well start working on
accepting it and being compassionate about it
now.

Just like we talked earlier about how little you know
and that you're going to make a lot of mistakes in life,
we now turn our attention to the fact that we will
frequently forget what we know and find ourselves
wandering around not sure what we're doing.

No matter your age, it can be hard to remember
what you know. At the same time, you will sometimes
surprise yourself about how many unimportant things
you remember quite clearly.

For example, there was a popular song from the early 1980's by Tommy Tutone that had a phone number
in it, and for some odd reason, I can remember that
number decades later, even though I never hear the
song anymore, "*...867-5309*." Meanwhile, I can't
remember the street address of our last home. How odd
is that?

All I'm saying here is that you're going to remember some things as you go through life but not be able to remember a lot of other things. Along the lines of forgetting things, let me ask you a series of questions:

Have you ever forgotten why you walked into a room?

Have you ever forgotten that your reading glasses were on top of your head?

Have you ever forgotten someone's name?

Have you ever forgotten a close friend's birthday?

Have you ever forgotten an appointment?

Have you ever forgotten how old you are?

Have you ever forgotten to pack something important for a trip?

Have you ever forgotten where you parked?

Have you ever forgotten to feed your fish?

Have you ever forgotten to pay a bill?

Have you ever forgotten where you put your car keys?

Have you ever forgotten your personal identification number?

Have you ever forgotten what you went to the store for?

Have you ever forgotten to thaw meat?

Have you ever forgotten to charge your cell phone?

Have you ever forgotten to flush?

Have you ever forgotten to zip your fly?

Have you ever forgotten to take your medicine?

Have your ever forgotten to take the trash out?

Have you ever forgotten to lock the front door to your home?

If you didn't say yes to all of these questions, you will someday. It's inevitable. Sooner or later, your memory is going to fade and you will forget things that you once remembered with no problem at all.

The most frustrating version of this for me is walking into a room and forgetting why I'm there. Lately, I've been doing a lot of remodeling around the house, and I can't tell you how many times I've walked into the garage to get something I need and can't remember what it was. I just kind of stand there for a minute or two, and if I can't pull it out of my memory bank, I go back in the house and see if something reminds me.

More often than not, going back in the house reminds of what I was looking for out in the garage, so I turn around and go to the garage as fast as I can so it doesn't slip my mind a second time. This is especially irritating when I am working upstairs, something that makes the back-and-forth trek longer and more of a pain in the butt.

Related to all this, I thought I was losing my mind at a popular home improvement chain store the other day. I had been shopping for about an hour and left my shopping cart in the aisle where the wood trim is to go looking for something else. When I came back, my shopping cart wasn't in the aisle where I left it. I initially thought I must have forgotten where I left my cart, so I walked the whole store looking for it (this was a big store, so it took a few minutes). My shopping cart wasn't anywhere in the store.

Now, I was really starting to freak out, because I was beginning to question whether or not I ever even had a shopping cart; it was about one step away from having a *Twilight Zone©* experience in which I began to question if I was even in that store shopping.

What I concluded was that an over-eager member of the store's staff must have found my cart, assumed someone had abandoned it, and put all the items back because the store was closing in fifteen minutes. That was a tad frustrating given that I had spent about an hour getting everything I needed. A first-world problem, for sure.

I'm kind of angry with that home improvement outlet right now because they recently re-organized their store. Now, I can't go right to the things I need anymore; I am having to re-learn where everything has been moved. At my age, I'm a tad sore that they didn't consult me before re-organizing their store, and sincerely hope this is the last time they will ever do that while I'm alive.

What are the things you forget the most often? Do you beat yourself up about it? Please don't. Stop shoulding all over yourself because to err is human, and it is also human to forget. Have compassion about the fact that you forget things fairly often in life. Let it be enough of a penalty that you had to make ten trips to the garage to finally get what you were looking for. Especially if you're doing things upstairs.

Chapter 11

I Should Be More Successful

*If at first you don't succeed, try, try
again. Then quit. There's no sense
in being a damn fool about it.*
—W.C. Fields

The idea that you can do anything you set your mind to and be a huge success in life is a load of baloney. It was devised by motivational speakers trying to sell you their self-improvement programs about how to make baloney sandwiches.

There are finite limitations all human beings have in the levels of intelligence, talent, ability, and drive we have when we come into the world; these are limitations that guarantee the vast majority of us will not be *huge* successes by human standards. Let me use my athletic career as a case in point.

I grew up playing baseball. I was a pretty good athlete but nothing to write home about. That didn't keep me from thinking I was going to be the starting pitcher for the New York Yankees. That never happened. Why? Because I wasn't athletically talented enough to play professional baseball.

In junior high school, I started playing tennis. I had dreams of playing on Centre Court at Wimbledon one day and winning the singles title. That never happened. Why? Because I wasn't athletically talented enough to play professional tennis, much less win a major singles title against uber-talented players.

In high school, I was my school's number one tennis player and had dreams of winning a district singles championship. Apparently, there were other players in the district who started playing tennis earlier than I did, took lessons along the way (I was self-taught), and had the same goal. Being the best singles player in my district never happened. Why? Because I wasn't a good enough tennis player to be the best in my district.

As an undergraduate at the University of Texas, I was delusional enough to try out for the tennis team as a walk-on. On the day of my tryout, I played another UT student who was trying out too. Under the watchful eye of the head coach, I proceeded to get my fanny kicked. I didn't make the team that day, nor did the kid who kicked my fanny. Why? Because neither of us were good enough tennis players to be on a Division I college tennis team.

While in college, I played tennis on a city league team named the "Woodshots." If I have to explain the name to you, you're obviously not a tennis player. Okay, we were called the "Woodshots" because racquets were made out of wood back then and sometimes you would hit the ball off the frame of your racquet. Wood-shots, get it?

Anyways, I was selected by the team to play the number one singles slot. To thank the team for having confidence in me, I hoped to win every match I played. I won more matches than I lost, but I wasn't the best singles player in the league. Why? Because I wasn't as good a player as some of the others in the league.

While in graduate school at the University of Texas, I was the assistant coach for the tennis team. From what I've said so far, you can safely assume that it wasn't because I was a great tennis player. I was the assistant coach because I was interested in sports psychology at the time and convinced the head coach I could teach the guys some things about "positive self-talk" that would help them win more matches.

I'll never forget the day I was at practice and a former player dropped by. He wasn't just any former player. He had won the NCAA singles title the year before, meaning he was the best player *in all of college tennis* that year.

He came to practice that day wanting to hit tennis balls with guys on the team if any were available. Unfortunately for him and me both, I was the only one available. So, we played a set against each other. Warning him that I was only the assistant tennis coach because of my psychology background, he spotted me a forty-love lead in every game. That meant he gave me a three-to-zero points lead to start each game and I was only one point away from winning every game we played. I didn't win one game.

One moment during the match was especially humiliating. This guy was known for his booming serve, hitting them so hard they would break the sound barrier as they crossed the net. He hit one serve so hard during our match that I could not get out of the way of it. I couldn't move fast enough to take it on the backhand or forehand side, and it hit me in the chest. I still have the dent to prove it.

I'm sure this guy must have thought the head coach had reached the bottom of the barrel to hire me as an assistant. That's why I told him before the match I was the assistant coach for my psychological skills, not my tennis skills.

I'm saying all this to you to make an important point: Whatever you feel called to do in life, please don't should all over yourself if you're not a huge success at it. Have compassion for yourself that compared to others who may be more talented, received better coaching, or worked just as hard as you have, you may never even crack the top ten in your local community at what you do. Just do whatever you do to the best of your ability. As they say in sports, leave it all out on the playing field so you can keep your head held high.

And, another thing: think about redefining what it means to be successful. Far too often, we define success in terms of what the scoreboard reads at the end of a game. May I suggest instead that we define success in terms of giving things our best shot and getting better over time. That's true success in life.

Now, I look back at trying out for the University of Texas tennis team differently. Rather than shoulding all over myself that I got my fanny kicked that day, I see it as a courageous effort to face the truth about where I stood as a tennis player at that point in my life.

There's no shame in that, even though I felt a lot of shame after having gotten so soundly trounced. I'm proud of the fact that I put my tennis skills on display so they could be evaluated by those in the know and so I wouldn't walk around the rest of my life being delusional enough to think I was going to win Wimbledon one day.

The old Army slogan is right: "Be all that you can be." Don't focus on being a huge success in how you compare to others, focus on fulfilling your own, unique potential. Focus on becoming a success in the sense that you left it all out there on the playing field and learned about where you need to improve.

Have compassion for yourself that very few people become huge successes in life by earthly standards; you may not have been blessed with enough talent, coaching, and ability to become one of them. Become a huge success in the right way by giving things all that you've got and being the gold medalist in getting better over time. The virtue really does lie in the struggle, not the prize.

Chapter 12

I Should Like Everything About the Way I Look

It's not the size of the nose that matters.
It's what's inside that counts.
—Steve Martin

Y ou don't need me to tell you that we are obsessed with external beauty in our world. As just one symptom of that, Americans spent $16.5 billion on cosmetic surgery in 2018. That's "billion" with a "b." Yikes!

Heaven forbid that you came into the world with a distinguishing physical feature the rest of the human race doesn't find attractive. How many of us have gone through life shoulding all over ourselves because we don't look like a model, a movie star, or a "hot" entertainer.

My earliest experience struggling with how I looked had to do with having acne as a teenager. Man, that was a rough time! Every zit led to feeling embarrassed. A bad outbreak led to not even wanting to go to school that day. Ugh, I shudder just to even think about it.

All this reminds me of a kid in high school who had an especially bad case of acne. Some of the kids in school called him "Pizza Face." My heart breaks for him when I think about the way he was treated about his acne, as if being in high school isn't inherently hard enough. How traumatic it must have been for him to be in school and know that some of his fellow students denigrated him because of his appearance.

My 50th high school reunion is coming up this Fall, and it triggers many memories of what it was like to be a high school student walking around feeling less than others just because you weren't as pretty or handsome.

I'm thankful I attended a high school that was full of fairly mature people who didn't put each other down about not being as attractive, smart, or athletic as those at the top of the class. But teenagers will be teenagers, and we were human enough to sometimes send out subtle and not-so-subtle signals that looks mattered and, unless you were a cut above the rest, you weren't quite as special.

In my high school, we doled out "Senior Superlatives," and, if I remember correctly, there was an award for handsomest and prettiest. Maybe they still do that today, but, frankly, I'd be surprised, given the emphasis on political correctness and how we are trying to be more careful about being *shallow* when comparing ourselves with others.

I must have been in denial about it most of my life, but it occurred to me a few years ago that I've got a big nose. It's not humongous, but it isn't small or average either. I never felt bad about my nose until that particular thought hit me. Now, every so often, I think to myself, *Man, you've got a honker for a nose!* and feel like I'm back in high school, embarrassed to walk down the hallways because I had an outbreak of acne that day.

On top of having a big nose, I've got a few more wrinkles on my face, less hair than I used to have, and my muscles are more like the Pillsbury Dough Boy™ than Rocky Balboa©. I'm not naturally a vain person (I hope) but getting older has been a big affront to whatever vanity I have. Recently, I stumbled across a website about how certain celebrities haven't aged all that well. It is beyond me why somebody felt a need to put something denigrating like that on the web.

If we could get past the issue of external beauty, we might be able to see that everyone is created in such a way that we would have to shield our eyes if we were to see the slightest glimpse of their beauty as fearfully and wonderfully made human beings.

I'm talking here about internal beauty, in the sense of being created with a mind, feelings, will, creativity, passions, abilities, and talents. That's real beauty. Everyone comes into the world fearfully and wonderfully made, and that is why everyone is beautiful, regardless how they feel on the inside or how others look at them from the outside.

So, the next time you start to should all over yourself that you don't meet the world's standards when it comes to how you look, tell the world to shove off. You are who you are, you look the way you look, and don't let anyone tell you that you're not beautiful in the way you are uniquely created as a human being.

I'm going to try and practice what I preach here by being proud of my nose. It's the one I came with, it's been serving me well for over six decades, and there's no reason to be ashamed of it. Besides, I've been poking that nose into other people's psychological business now for 40 years and getting paid for doing it. That's nothing to be embarrassed about.

Chapter 13

I Should Be Emotionally Smarter

If your emotional abilities aren't in hand, if you don't have self-awareness, if you are not able to manage your distressing emotions, if you can't have empathy and have effective relationships, then no matter how smart you are, you are not going to get very far.
—Daniel Goleman

Emotional intelligence is a term coined by researchers in the 1990's that refers to being aware of your own feelings and the feelings of others, handling your emotions in an appropriate manner, channeling your emotions in the direction of your goals while being able to delay gratification in the process, having empathy toward others in terms of being able to understand their feelings and points of view, and having healthy social skills that enable you to help others manage their emotions better.

In light of what emotional intelligence is, we're all emotionally unintelligent to some degree when it comes how well we understand ourselves and interact with others. To put it differently, we all struggle to attach to others in a safe and secure manner. Sure, some people are better at it than others, but even the people who are good at it can be pretty left-footed at times when it comes to how they interact with others. For most of us, it's a daily challenge to grow in our emotional intelligence over time so we finish life better at interpersonal relationships than when we started.

I was blessed to have a loving mom and dad growing up, both of whom have passed away. As I look back on the two of them, it saddens me that they weren't taught by their parents how to be emotionally intelligent and develop close relationships with others. Sure, their parents taught them to work hard, act morally, and be a model citizen, but they were never shown how to have intimate relationships with others.

Consequently, they didn't know how to bond on a deep level with each other as husband and wife, or how to help me bond with them, my three brothers, or other people in my life. It certainly wasn't malicious or intentional on their part, it was just the effect of unhealthy relational skills being painfully passed from one generation to the next.

Given that I was an introspective, sensitive, and relationally-oriented kid growing up, I noticed this more and more about my family as I got older. When I was growing up in our house, it seemed it was all mostly about doing your chores, making good grades, having good table manners, and not doing anything to embarrass your family. That's all well and good, but it didn't teach me how to interact with and be close to others, something that led to not being all that emotionally intelligent when I left home.

When the time came, I went off to college and chose to attend the University of Texas, one of the largest schools in the nation at the time in terms of the size of the student body (48,000 on-campus students). It was no accident I chose to go to Texas. I was probably unconsciously thinking I could disappear into the crowd while I was there, in terms of not having to get to know anyone on a deeper level, even though that was what my heart longed for. My emotional intelligence was still pretty low at that time, so I went through my undergraduate program not getting to know anyone all that well or allowing anyone to get to know me very well, either. Of course, I majored in psychology.

I then went off to graduate school to get a master's degree in, of course, counseling. I still found myself keeping everyone at arm's length in terms of developing a healthy closeness with classmates or the students in the dorm where I was an assistant head resident. I still didn't have a clue as to how to break through the wall I had erected with others and develop a close connection. I got my degree and left.

I went from there to the University of Tennessee to be the head resident of one of their dorms, still keeping mostly to myself, making friends where I could, but not really getting to know anyone particularly well. I think that was the most relationally lonely and empty year of my life. Thinking I would be there for a couple of years or longer, I left after one year.

I went back to the University of Texas to work on a doctorate in, you guessed it, counseling psychology. My fellow doctoral students were a great group of people, and the professors had a genuine interest in training us to be competent psychologists. Still, I continued my "keep 'em at arm's length" style of relating to others, not really getting to know anyone all that well.

While working on my doctorate, I met and married my wife, Holly. As I had done to everyone else in my life, I didn't know how to be emotionally close to her; I tended to stay busy all the time so I didn't ever have to face that fact. Holly, being the gracious and patient person she is, has hung in there with me and hasn't given up on her vision that the two of us can pull off a level of closeness that goes beyond what either of us witnessed in our families growing up. As I write these words, we are four days away from our 40th wedding anniversary, so she has been patient a long, long time.

With the birth of our children, I continued to run into how uncomfortable I was with being close to people, even my own children. I turned out to be the same kind of father my Dad was, a driven, achievement-oriented, Type A who was focused way too much on his career and not enough on being close with his own wife and children. Still, my psychological bent helped me to be a more engaged father than what I had experienced growing up.

As I head into my sunset years, I'm still uncomfortable with closeness, but I'm doing much better. I go on more walks with my wife, call my kids more often, rather than waiting for them to call me, tell my close friends how much I care about them, love up on and listen to my clients more deeply, and am currently forming a healthy bond with my precious granddaughters and grandson. While I still have a lot of work ahead of me, I am more emotionally intelligent about how interpersonal relationships work and more excited about the future than I have ever been.

What I'm saying is, most of us have what we psychologists call "attachment issues;" we find it hard to develop deep levels of closeness with others. I don't say that to discourage anyone. I say it to challenge all of us to not should all over ourselves because we struggle to overcome the barriers that get in the way of bonding with others. I want us to have compassion for ourselves and others about this human dilemma and work out our relational salvation together.

Reach out to the people you love, who love you back, and spend the rest of your life trying to work through your attachment issues with them. Do it with as much grace, compassion, patience, and forgiveness as you can, regardless of the fact that very few of us know what we are doing, even we psychologist types.

Don't should all over yourself if your emotional intelligence is low and drawing close to others scares the starch out of your shirts. Welcome to the planet. Be compassionate toward yourself and everyone else you know, because we're all in the same boat together. Let's stay committed to working on improving our emotional intelligence so we won't look back with regret that we kept people at arm's length while we were here.

Chapter 14

I Should Be in a Better Mood

*You know sometimes when you're in a
really bad mood and you're not sure
why? That's how I get sometimes.*
—Masie Williams

There's a funny line in the movie, *Steel Magnolias*©. One of the lead characters in the film is a crotchety old woman named Ouiser (pronounced "Wee-zur"), played by Shirley MacLaine. At one point in the movie, overprotective mother, M'Lynn, played by Sally Fields, questions Ouiser's mental health. Ouiser's pithy response was, "I'm not crazy, M'Lynn. I've just been in a very bad mood for 40 years!"

I identify with Ouiser. On the day I wrote these words, I turned 67. I feel like I've been in a bad mood since I was 17, so I've been in a bad mood for 50 years, much longer that Ouiser! It ain't a lot of fun, I can tell you, but it is what it is.

The two emotions I have struggled with in my life have been sadness and anger. It's hard to look back to a time in the past when I didn't feel both sad and angry. I've always had a bad temper, something I think I got from my paternal grandfather, who was reported to have once struck a horse in the face with his fist because it wasn't cooperating with him. And I've always been "blue," largely because I have an "Eeyore" personality and everything looks dark and gloomy.

Not a great combination, right? Right.

My anger typically came out on the sports field growing up. I played tennis for twenty-five years until my late thirties, and I can't begin to tell you how many racquets I broke when I was playing. Remember, back in my day, racquets were made out of wood. You don't have to bang a wood racquet on the ground very hard to splinter it into a million pieces. Whether it was missing an easy shot, getting a bad line call, or the wind pushing a well-hit shot out of bounds, it didn't take much to trigger an explosion of anger out of me, right there in public view.

My sadness isn't really triggered by anything in particular, it's just always been there. It doesn't seem to matter how good my circumstances are, I'm just always sad. Like Eeyore, it always seems to be cloudy and gray in my soul.

That I'm always angry and sad could be a trigger for self-condemnation, something I have been pretty good at when my anger boils over or I can't snap myself out of being blue. Being self-condemning about it has only made things worse. I decided some time ago to work on having compassion for myself for having anger and depression issues and keep on doing the best I can to not allow either to dictate how I live my life.

Bad moods are part of life. You might be a happy-go-lucky person who is rarely in a bad mood. If you are, I'm happy for you. You are blessed to have the kind of personality and brain chemistry that make your life more emotionally enjoyable. For those of us on the other end of the continuum, the ones whose personalities and brain chemistry seem to be doing everything they can to make our lives emotionally difficult, it's more challenging to keep our heads above water each day.

A quick caveat: I've been talking so far about *overly strong* feelings of sadness and anger. Don't forget, when we experience something like the death of a loved one or the loss of a job, we're supposed to feel sad. When someone cuts you off in traffic and shoots you the finger, you're supposed to feel angry. We tend to call sadness, anger, hurt, and anxiety "negative" emotions, but they aren't. They're just painful.

So, when these kinds of life events come your way, let yourself feel sad, angry, and anxious. Be in a "bad" mood. Just make sure you don't allow these painful emotions to become so intense that they overwhelm you; don't hold on to them so long that they negatively impact the rest of your life.

If you're like Ouiser and me, you've been in a bad (painful) mood most of your life. Be kind to yourself about it. Try to have empathy and compassion because, emotionally, you've been pushing a boulder uphill the whole time before you go to the Great Beyond.

Remember, treat yourself the way you would treat your best friend if he or she was in a bad mood. You wouldn't beat them up or condemn them, right? You wouldn't say to them, "You shouldn't be feeling this way and need to snap out of it," right? You would have compassion for the emotional pain they were in, offer comfort, and encourage them to keep their head up and do whatever they can to come out of it. Treat yourself like you would treat them, so you can emotionally keep your head above water and ultimately get on dry land and start feeling good again.

Chapter 15

I Should Know What I Want
To Do with My Life

Today is the first day of the rest of your life, and if
you screw that up, you can start again tomorrow.
—Ingrid Weir

I am pretty fortunate in that I knew, early on, I
wanted to be a psychologist. I knew when I was a
freshman in high school and actually wrote a letter
to the American Psychological Association for information on how to become one. I'm pretty fortunate.

While I had a clear sense of what I wanted to be
when I grew up, I experienced a bump in the road early
on. It almost discouraged me to not pursue my professional dream.

The first psychology class I took in college, *Introduction to Psychology*, had, I'm guessing, over 400 students in
it. That foundational class was taught by a professor
who was at least 150 years old and should have been put
out to academic pasture years earlier. I had never been
in a class that large, hadn't learned how to perform well
on multiple choice tests, and proceeded to make a D in
the class. Did I say it was *Introduction to Psychology*?

Obviously, my career as a psychologist didn't get off
to a rousing start, and I had moments of doubt along

the way about whether I was ever going to become one. I decided to stay the course, not worry about whether my grades would be good enough to get me into graduate school, and the rest is history.

Because I knew so early what I wanted to do with my life professionally, I'm not going to draw from personal experience in this chapter. I'm going to draw from the experience of the clients with whom I have had the privilege of working, who *didn't* know what they wanted to do. The person I'm about to introduce you to is a composite of numerous clients I've counseled; specifics have been altered to protect their identities.

Tom grew up in a home in which higher education was greatly valued. Even though neither of his parents had college degrees, it was clear from the start that he was going to go to college and "make something of himself," whether he wanted to or not. That was all well and good, but Tom had no earthly idea what he wanted to do job-wise.

Tom went off to college not knowing what to major in, so he decided to major in general studies, figuring that something would grab him along the way. Nothing did. Along the way, he switched from general studies to physical education, thinking he would become a high school teacher and baseball coach. That didn't light his fire, so he switched to computer science, thinking he might work for a tech company. That didn't work out, and Tom finally settled on majoring in construction management.

Once he got his degree, Tom went to work for a construction company with an eye toward ultimately becoming a project manager. After years of working for the company, he still isn't sure if construction management is his cup of tea, but he is going to stay with it until he becomes a project manager to see if that works out for him.

My heart breaks for Tom. He is a smart, hard-working and responsible person who is doing the best he can to put a roof over his family's head, but he has to drag himself out of bed most days and do a job he doesn't enjoy all that much and isn't sure is a good fit for him.

He tends to get down on himself about all this, often saying, "I should have all this figured out by now and can't believe I'm not settled in a career." On top of that, he's pretty sure everyone else on the planet has their careers figured out and they all hop out of bed each day with big smiles on their faces and a click in their heels.

Tom's path through life seems to be the more common one these days. I wish we counselor-types had an occupational MRI machine we could run people through so we could tell them when they're young exactly what job would be the best match for them. Sadly, there's no such machine, and most people have to bounce around a little bit (some have to bounce around a lot) until they find their occupational sweet spot. My hat's off to anyone doing honorable work in an effort to provide for their families until they find what they're looking for professionally.

There are days as a psychologist when I wonder if I chose the right career path. Sometimes the pressure and heaviness of helping people handle the emotional pain they're in is daunting. Sometimes, I'll go home and want to be completely left alone with only a diet soda and the remote to deal with. But every job, no matter how much we are called to do it, is like that. I'd rather be dealing with that kind of emotional exhaustion than dealing with the emotional exhaustion of not knowing what I want to do in life.

If you're out there still bouncing around from one thing to another, looking for what lights your fire, I want you to stop shoulding all over yourself about it. Keep your head up that you're doing the best you can and have compassion for yourself (and others) that you still haven't found what you're looking for. And I want you to keep looking, because, who knows, you just might find it someday. If you don't, at least you tried.

Chapter 16

I Shouldn't Have Bad Habits

A habit is something you can do without thinking-
which is why most of us have so many of them.
—Frank A. Clarke

I didn't know it until I began writing this chapter, but there are a lot of "bad habits" lists on the internet. One list said that the top ten bad habits that offend others the most are: being more than five minutes late for an appointment; picking your nose; over-the-top public displays of affection (PDAs); picking your teeth; overusing slang and "text speak"; checking your cell phone at dinner; eating with your mouth open; having alligator arms (never picking up checks); popping/snapping gum in public; and talking during movies.[3]

One of my bad habits throughout my life has been biting my fingernails, something I continue to do to this day. My mom was so bothered by this habit when I was a young boy that she bought this horrible tasting product that she would brush on my fingernails to discourage me from biting them. I don't know if she got tired of doing it or she knew it was a lost cause, because I would bite them anyway, so her efforts to stop me from biting my nails didn't last very long.

---

[3] https://www.developgoodhabits.com/list-of-bad-habits/

I think biting my nails growing up was a coping mechanism for all the anxiety I felt as a kid and have continued to feel as an adult. In some strange way, it is how I comfort myself. It reminds me of another habit I had as a kid, rocking myself to sleep. When I was a boy, I couldn't fall asleep at night unless I rocked back and forth, another coping mechanism for the anxiety I must have felt at the time. I didn't stop rocking myself to sleep until I got to the end of elementary school, whereas biting my nails still goes on.

Not to gross you out, but I had another bad habit as a kid, picking my nose. Frankly, I don't know very many kids who don't do this, but it is a particularly nasty habit. To be honest, I enjoyed picking my nose as a kid and then joining my buddies in trying to put the choicest buggers on each other's clothes.

My two precious granddaughters pick their noses. They can't seem to pick their noses enough lately. I told my oldest granddaughter that her head was going to cave in if she kept mining her nose for buggers. She knows I joke a lot, so she very rarely takes anything I say seriously.

My youngest granddaughter actually wiped a bugger on me the other day. She thought it was hilarious, while I didn't find it all that funny. I would have never wiped a bugger on my grandparents when I was a kid, but we live in a different age now where everything kids or grandkids do is the funniest thing imaginable.

That same granddaughter also loves to burp. She's come up with some sonic boom burps in her short lifetime. I can only hope, by the time she joins civilized society, she will have brought her nose picking and burp production to a halt.

A nasty habit I cannot stand in others is eating with your mouth open. For me, that is like nails on a chalkboard. My Mom raised her four sons to have manners; we were never allowed to put our elbows on the dinner table, our feet on the coffee table, track dirt into the house, leave our dirty clothes laying around, sit nine feet away from the dinner table, or chew food with our mouths open. All of those were cardinal sins in our family, and Mom wasn't about to let us do anything like that.

That's how Mom did it and that's how I did it with my kids. God love 'em, but dinner was not always a pleasant experience in the Thurman family. I got on my kids all the time about their table manners, and I also didn't allow them to say "yea," "huh," or "What?" when they interacted with Holly and me. They had to say "Yes, ma'am," "Excuse me," and "I'm sorry, I didn't quite get that. Could you say it again, please?" Come heck or high water, I was going to raise my kids to have good manners and not any nasty habits.

Given that kids have free will, something I wish they didn't have, each of my three kids has grown up to be their own person. While they are not wild savages by any stretch of the imagination, they haven't maintained many of the good habits I taught them, except chewing with their mouths closed and using utensils rather than their hands to eat. Don't get me started on their potty mouths. But my kids are all in their thirties now, so I can't do anything about it. That's why I'm currently turning my attention to my granddaughters. Come heck or high water.

The point I'm trying to make is that we all have some nasty habits we engage in and I don't want us shoulding all over ourselves about it. Most of the time, nasty habits are a coping mechanism for dealing with the stress and anxiety we feel (or a sign that we weren't raised properly--sorry, I'm only the messenger). So, don't beat yourself up for having nasty habits, just be more sensitive to the fact that those around you might be somewhat bothered if you chew with your mouth open, arrive five to ten minutes late, pick your nose, talk over them, pick your teeth, use your cell phone at dinner, overuse slang, publicly express too much affection, pop your gum, talk during movies, or any of the other 283 bad habits listed on the web.[4]

Be compassionate with yourself that you've developed some bad habits over the years but keep trying to be more socially aware of their impact on others. You don't want to drive people away by chewing with your mouth open when you're around them, right?

---

[4] https://www.developgoodhabits.com/list-of-bad-habits/

Chapter 17

I Shouldn't Be Losing a Step

Life begins at 40 – but so do fallen arches, rheumatism, faulty eyesight and the tendency to tell a story to the same person, three or four times.
—Helen Rowland

Have you ever heard the expression, "You're no spring chicken anymore"? It's usually meant in the negative, that someone is getting older, isn't looking as good, isn't functioning as well, and is well past their prime. It can be a way we put others down for getting older and losing a step or two along the way.

My favorite comedian when it comes to talking about getting older is George Burns, someone who lived to be 100 years old. We should all live that long. Here's my top ten list of Burns' funniest observations about getting older.

* "First you forget names, then you forget faces. Next you forget to pull your zipper up and finally, you forget to pull it down."

* "I get up every morning and read the obituary column. If my name's not there, I eat breakfast."

* "You know you're getting old when you stoop to tie your shoelaces and wonder what else you could do while you're down there."

* "If you live to be one hundred, you've got it made. Very few people die past that age."

* "I'd rather be over the hill than under it."

* "I'm very pleased to be here. Let's face it, at my age I'm very pleased to be anywhere."

* "At my age flowers scare me."

* "You can't help getting older, but you don't have to get old."

* "When you stop giving and offering something to the rest of the world, it's time to turn out the lights."

* "Young. Old. Just words. Inside we feel like our shoe size."

Finally, when asked what he wanted printed on his gravestone, George Burns said: "I want it to say, 'I wish I could be standing here reading this.'"

What a great attitude. I wish that had been my attitude along the way. All I find myself doing is a lot of whining, moaning, and complaining about getting older.

The first clear indication of my getting older emerged on the day I turned 40; it seemed my eyesight immediately worsened. I had never worn glasses in my whole life before 40, but I have been wearing reading glasses ever since.

The second sign I was getting older was that my hair began to thin. When I got a haircut, they sprayed water on my hair and start cutting, but at 40 and beyond, I began seeing a different ratio of scalp to hair. I saw a lot more of my scalp on top of my head than I cared to.

The third indicator I was getting older was noticing that I was beginning to have old man's hands. The backs of my hands began to freckle and didn't look as good as they had. It's not the case I ever was one, but it was painfully obvious I would never be a hand model in the future.

The fourth sign I was getting older was that my hearing began to go south. I attributed this to listening to way too much rock music at a way too high volume my whole life, but the loss may have had nothing to do with that. Now, with significant hearing loss in my left ear and mild hearing loss in my right, I have to ask people to repeat things a lot and Holly has to walk on my right side when we take our evening stroll.

The fifth "aging factor" I noticed was having less energy. I used to be able to play a round of golf, stay out in the yard doing yardwork, and work out at the gym for hours – all on the same day. Now, after a round of golf, a few hours in the yard, and 30 minutes on the exercise bike, all on different days, I'm ready to call it a day.

The sixth variable in my aging was noticing that I have a lot more aches and pains. I blame some of this on still having the same mattress we've had for 100 years; you know, the kind of mattress that has the Grand Canyon winding its way down the middle of it. Whatever is causing it, my body hurts a lot more than it used to.

I'm not whining here (I hope). I'm just trying to encourage you to not get down on yourself when you begin to lose a step and aren't a Spring chicken anymore. Just like death and taxes are inescapable, so is the aging process. Be kind to yourself when your eyesight fades, hearing goes, hair thins, hands freckle, energy decreases, and aches and pains keep you from movin' very fast. You may not be resonating with any of this now, but I can assure you, you will later on.

This weekend I'm going to put mulch in my flower beds. I'm not looking forward to it because I have to drive over to the big home improvement store, buy a bunch of big honking bags of mulch, load them in my car, drive home, unload them in my driveway, open them up one-by-one, put mulch in the flower beds one scoop at a time, and stoop or bend down on the ground, over and over, to do it. I'm getting tired just thinking about it.

Getting older and losing a step are inevitable, but, keep in mind, you're about as old *internally* as you let yourself be. As Jack Benny put it, "Age is strictly a case of mind over matter. If you don't mind, it doesn't matter." We really can stay as young in heart and mind as we care to be. Just because our body is experiencing the ravages of time, doesn't mean we have to cede our spirit.

As you get older, don't should all over yourself that you're losing a step along the way. Everyone does. Just make sure you stay physically active and young at heart attitudinally and keep telling Father Time to bug off. If we do, maybe we'll live to be 100 years old like George Burns.

Chapter 18

I Shouldn't Have a Bad Bent

Evil things are easy: for they are natural to our fallen nature. Right things are rare flowers that need cultivation.
—Charles Spurgeon

The debate about human nature has been around for a long time. Some psychologists, philosophers, and theologians will tell you that human nature is basically good; it just needs to be brought out and encouraged. Others will tell you that people are naturally inclined toward the bad, and we have to fight that inclination the whole time we're here.

I agree with the folks in the second camp. Before you get upset, I'm not talking about the issue of *worth* here. From my perspective, everyone has worth, no one having less or more than any other human being. Here, I'm talking about whether or not it's our natural inclination to do good or our natural inclination to do bad.

I tell my clients that we all come with three fallen bents as human beings: selfishness (the tendency to take rather than give); laziness (the tendency to cut corners when it comes to the hard work we need to do to grow and mature); and immaturity (the tendency to act like a five-year-old when life gets in the way of what we want). I call these three the "unholy trinity." They are powerfully and actively in you from the day you draw your first breath to the day you let out your last.

It's not our fault that we're bent these three ways. None of us woke up one day as kids and said, "You know, I think I'll be selfish, lazy and immature the rest of my life so I can drive myself and everyone else crazy." No, you came by it naturally. It is what it is.

As much as we say children are precious and wonderful, and they are, they come into the world selfish, lazy, and immature. I don't say this to put them down, they just are. Having raised three kids, I can speak from personal experience. For the most part, all my ankle biters did when they were little was be selfish, lazy, and immature. How could they have been any other way?

Left up to their own devices, all that young kids would do all day long is play, eat sweets, go to the bathroom, burp, put buggers on you, and watch five hundred cartoons. As parents or grandparents, when we interrupt any of these activities and demand that they do unpleasant things (eat green beans, pick up their toys, do their homework, brush their teeth, take a bath, etc.), they throw an absolute hissy fit because all their selfish, lazy, immature fun has to end.

Think about a baby on day one. All they're doing is thinking about themselves and what they want (selfish), expecting you to feed them and change their horrible-smelling diapers (lazy), and screaming and yelling when they don't get their way (immature). When people say our nature is basically good, they either don't remember their own childhood, have never had kids, or have had kids but still have serious delusions that their kids are precious little angels.

You may be ready to throw this book across the room, but before you do, let me say something even more offensive. The majority of people don't improve much when it comes to overcoming these three bad bents. Very few people are *significantly* less selfish, lazy or immature by the time they go to the Great Beyond. I like how Bryan White put it, "We never really grow up, we only learn how to act in public."

From my perspective, the majority of us really don't mature much, we simply learn how to act in public. That's why it's truly impressive when someone becomes a noticeably more selfless, hard-working, and mature person as they get older. It's a rare phenomenon and they are to be praised for pulling it off.

Nothing will reveal our natural fallenness to us more than being married. I think, for a lot of couples, the "empty nest" years are as hard as they are because once you are no longer distracted by your selfish, lazy, and immature kids, you have to face how selfish, lazy, and immature you and your spouse have been throughout your marriage.

Given that we tend to see our spouse as the one who is *worse*, some of us become bitter and resentful and start thinking the grass is greener with someone else. It's not. Anyone you find is going to be just as selfish, lazy, and immature as you and your ex-spouse were. As Joyce Meyer put it, "Even if you think the grass is greener on the other side, you're going to have to mow that side too."

I'm crazy about my kids. To me, they are a wonderful gift that keeps on giving. I gotta tell you, though, they came into the world selfish, lazy, and immature, and they are going to leave the world selfish, lazy, and immature, just like I will. Like all of us, they will continue fighting these three fallen bents throughout their lives, and that is why we need to bathe them and ourselves in as much compassion, grace, and encouragement as we possibly can

As Mark Twain put it, "Everyone is a moon, and has a dark side which he never shows to anybody." Don't should all over yourself that you have a dark side, just admit to it, open up to others about it, and work to grow and mature as much as you can.

A very wise person, Paul of Tarsus, once said, "When I was a child, I talked like a child, I thought like a child, I reasoned like a child. When I became a man, I put the ways of childhood behind me" (1 Corinthians 13:11). I think that pretty much sums up one of the major challenges of life: Going from being selfish, lazy, and immature as kids, to being selfless, hard-working, and mature as adults; getting to the point of putting childish ways behind us.

Don't should all over yourself if you haven't made that transition yet, but don't make any excuses either. The world needs more adults around, not a bunch of large, petulant children. Let's work hard to put childish ways behind us so we can make the world a better place.

Chapter 19

I Should Be a Better Communicator

*The single biggest problem with communication
is the illusion that it has taken place.*
—**George Bernard Shaw**

I may have mentioned I'm doing a lot of home improvement projects lately. I can't remember if I wrote that earlier because I sometimes forget things. That's something I'm trying to bathe in self-compassion, rather than self-condemnation and shaming myself.

Recently, we had a water leak behind our washer and dryer that soaked a small section of sheetrock. Rather than pay someone to replace the sheetrock, I started licking my lips because this was another opportunity for me to add to my ever-expanding repertoire of home improvement skills. So, I decided to do it myself. Big mistake.

I can't begin to tell you the amount of mayhem that replacing a small section of sheetrock created in my life.

First, it was a huge mess to pull all the damp plasterboard off the wall. Second, I had to go to the big home improvement store to get the replacement sheetrock. Since I don't have a truck or a big car, I had to cut out the replacement section in its exact size because I couldn't fit an entire 4'X8' piece in my car. So, I had to buy a box cutter, throw a big, honking 4' by 8' piece of sheetrock on top of a cart as a workbench, measure the section I needed, "score" it, bend and break it into the pieces I needed, and take all the various pieces home with me.

As if that weren't bad enough, I didn't cut the pieces right and had to do some further cutting when I got home. This turned my garage into a blowy, white winter wonderland. To add further insult to injury, I cut the most important piece a little too long. Rather than take it back into the garage to cut it the right length, I tried to jam it into the space where it was supposed to go and damaged the sheetrock. Consequently, I had to go back to the big home improvement store and buy a lot of spackling to repair the damage.

On top of all that, I needed to match the texture of the newly inserted sheetrock to the texture of the sheetrock that didn't need to be removed. So, I went back to the big home improvement store again to try to see what I could find. Unfortunately, this was where my less-than-wonderful communication skills came into play.

I asked one of the helpful salespeople if they had any texture one could spray on sheetrock. He had the gall to ask me what type of texture I was looking for. Apparently, since there are with so many items at the big home improvement store, there also are a million versions of wall texture.

I foolishly embarked on an effort to describe the wall texture I was looking for:

"You know, it's like the landscape of the moon. No, it's more like a pimply-faced kid. No, it's got a lot of bumps on it. Well, maybe it's more like…"

The salesperson, trying to hang in there with me as long as he could, stopped me, and marched me over to the area where all the spray texture was (as if he couldn't have done that already and saved me from embarrassing myself). He then asked me if I saw anything that remotely looked like the wall texture I had at home. Sure enough, I spotted what I needed (by the way, it's called "orange peel" as if I was supposed to know that), bought two cans, and went on my merry way, much to the salesperson's delight.

Sometimes product manufacturers lie to us. I followed the instructions on the spray texture can to a "t." I sprayed on the texture, let it dry for a few minutes, then scraped it just like the can said. Unfortunately, on the newly sheet rocked and sprayed wall, the texture didn't look anything like orange peel, or any other citrus rind.

So, I went back to the big home improvement store, bought a texture I could apply with a brush, and resolved to solve my problem with that approach. Unfortunately, the texture I painted on the wall looks nothing like anything already on the wall. I now have two noticeably different wall textures in my small cubby-hole of a washer-dryer area. I'm thankful the new sheetrock is down low behind the washer and dryer where nobody can see it. Harken back to my, "I am a compulsive neat freak," declaration. Nuff said.

I don't know if you're like me, but I think a lot of us should all over ourselves because we aren't great communicators. If you're like me, you get tongue-tied fairly often, start saying way too many words, and get further and further off the highway of clear communication about what you're trying to say. Don't beat yourself up about that. Great communication skills are a rare commodity. Most of us are just faking it.

This book you hold in your hands is another example of what I'm talking about. As much as I'm trying to communicate to you in the clearest way I can about the deadly effects of shoulding all over yourself, I have fumbled around a lot; I constantly rewrote what I wrote. Sometimes, I went back to a previous chapter and wondered if I had bumped my head right before I wrote it, because it didn't make a dang bit of sense.

I think this is why I love reading books and watching movies where a great communicator is doing his or her thing. Man, when some of those people get going, it's like the most beautiful symphony you've ever heard. Ah, to communicate like they do would be a wonderful thing.

Please, don't should all over yourself that your communication skills may not be the best on the planet. Just keep trying to communicate with others as best you can. Along the way, if you get that "deer in the headlamp, I have no earthly idea what you're talking about" stare from the person you're talking to, take a deep breath and try again.

I still go to that big home improvement store, so I often get that "I don't know what you're talking about" look from the salespeople, but they are always patient as I fumble around trying to describe what I need. On occasion, I've been so bad at describing what I need that I'm not even talking about anything they have in the store. So, I try again, because I know they have it *somewhere*.

Look, I have three college degrees and I'm a psychologist, but there are times I can't rub two coherent sentences together. If I had a nickel for every time someone looked at me like I was a babbling idiot, I would be a wealthy man. Have compassion on yourself, because it is not easy being clear and articulate when talking to others; we all need to cut each other a lot of slack about it.

Chapter 20

I Shouldn't Have Unlikeable Qualities

Some people are inherently likeable. If you're not,
work on it. It may even improve your social life.
—Antonin Scalia

ll of us come into the world with some likeable
and some unlikeable qualities. For many of us,
it's our unlikeable qualities we are the most
concerned about, especially when we are exposing them
to a watchful world and hoping people don't react with
criticism or condemnation. Because we're afraid of
revealing our unlikeable qualities, we often hide too
much of ourselves from others, rather than risk being
who we are and letting the chips fall where they may.

Among my dislikeable qualities, I think the one I am
most self-condemning about is how negative I can be.
Way too often, I find my mind wandering over to the
negative, dark, worst-case scenario side of the street
regarding how I look at myself and others. The glass
isn't half empty to me, it often doesn't have any water in
it at all. It's broken. That once-full glass is drenched
shards.

All this may have a familiar ring to it if you're a
"Winnie the Pooh©" fan. In the world of Winnie the
Pooh, as I've said, I'm Eeyore. I *am* that sad-sack don-

key who always thinks the sky is falling and everything is going to hell in a handbasket. Here are my top-ten favorite Eeyore statements about how Eeyore (and I) views things:

> "It's not much of a tail, but I'm sort of attached to it."
>
> "The nicest thing about the rain is that it always stops. Eventually."
>
> "Wish I could say yes, but I can't."
>
> "After all, what are birthdays? Here today and gone tomorrow."
>
> "Sure is a cheerful color. I guess I'll have to get used to it."
>
> "I'd say thistles, but nobody listens to me, anyway."
>
> "It's all for naught."
>
> "Most likely, lose it again anyway."
>
> "If it's a good morning, which I doubt."
>
> "Nobody tells me. Nobody keeps me informed. I make it 17 days come Friday since anybody spoke to me."[5]

You can tell from these statements that Eeyore doesn't exactly have a chipper attitude about life. It's a wonder Eeyore has any friends. His best friend is Tigger, the happy-go-lucky tiger, who joyfully bounces from one place to another. Thank goodness for the Tiggers in life. If it weren't for them, we Eeyores wouldn't have any friends other than other Eeyores who would simply join us in our doom-and-gloom view of life.

---

[5] https://einsteinquotes.org/eeyore-quotes/

Let me give you a recent example of how negative I can be. I'm a Texas Longhorn fan. In the midst of the coronavirus pandemic, I was (negatively) afraid my beloved Longhorns weren't going to get to play football in the 2020 season. Thankfully, they were cleared to play and had their first game against the University of Texas-El Paso.

Prior to the game, I was (negatively) sure they were going to lay an egg against a more-than-beatable opponent. In the past, the 'Horns have had a bad habit of doing that; I was (negatively) sure they were going to crush my dreams again by not winning all the winnable games. Thankfully, they played really well and came away with an impressive win, getting the season off to a good start. The Longhorns beat the UTEP Miners 59-3.

Still, that didn't keep me, Dr. Negative, from finding something to be bothered about. Here's my negative list about how the game turned out: We didn't score enough points (we actually scored 59 points and beat the spread, which is dang good); we allowed our opponent to score too many points (our opponent only scored 3 points, which was really good); we gave up too many yards on defense (the other team only had 233 total yards of offense, which is pretty good); we didn't have enough yards of offense (we had 683 yards of offense, which is really good, especially since we took our foot off the gas and played second and third stringers in the second half); and we only got one turnover (an interception).

I guess I would have only been happy if we had scored 150 points, kept them to zero points, rolled up a thousand yards of offense, kept them to five yards of offense (still too many), had six interceptions and five fumble recoveries, and kept them from ever crossing mid-field or picking up a first down. I think you get the point. The game I watched most recently could have been a good moment for me as a fan, if I weren't so dang negative.

As you can tell, I'm even negative about my negativity. It is no fun being the kind of person who can suck the last iota of positivity out of what could have been a good moment in life. Negativity gets in the way of enjoying when things go well, appreciating that they did, and being more optimistic about life.

As you go through life, I want you to stop shoulding all over yourself about your unlikeable traits. Keep trying to move in the direction of your likeable ones, not in an unhealthy effort to be liked by everyone, but to become a more well-rounded human being. To help you along, here are some *likeable* traits you might want to work on:

*You're accountable for your mistakes.
*You're optimistic without being unrealistic.
*You do what you say you will do.
*You can laugh at yourself.
*You treat everyone with respect.
*You don't exaggerate.
*You ask questions instead of making assumptions.
*You're not afraid to be vulnerable.
*You follow-up on things.
*You don't interrupt.
*You smile.
*You're consistent.

*You remember people's names.

*You admit when you're wrong.

*You offer to help.

*You aren't afraid to make mistakes.

*You let others do most of the talking.

*You send thank you notes.

*You maintain good eye contact.

*You encourage others.

*You give others your undivided attention.

*You apologize when you mess up.

*You don't criticize, condemn, or shame others.

*You forgive others when they hurt you.

*You know how to give and receive a compliment.

*You celebrate others' successes.

*You tell the truth.[6]

A pretty daunting list, isn't it? If you want a list of unlikeable qualities, just put the word "don't" after "You" and the word "not" after "You're" in each statement. Take a minute to look through the list. Pick out a few likeable traits you are going try to work on in how you interact with others.

I'm going to work harder on being realistically optimistic and smile a lot more. Having spent my life frowning too much and seeing things in a pessimistic light, I'm excited about changing in this better and more life-enhancing manner. I think those around me will be excited about it, too.

Please, don't should all over yourself that you have more than a few unlikeable traits. Don't shame or con-

---

[6] https://www.inc.com/andrew-thomas/39-extraordinary-traits-of-likable-people.html

demn yourself that, like everyone else on the planet, there are things about you that are disagreeable and turn others off. Have compassion that your unlikeable traits have harmed you as a human being and harmed your relationships with others. work on internalizing likeable traits as the way you want to be when you're interacting with others. Do it for yourself from a personal growth perspective, and do it for others so you will be more enjoyable to be around.

Chapter 21

I Should Have High Self-Esteem

He should be the utmost of honesty, generosity,
considerateness, justice, dignity, courage,
unselfishness. He should be the perfect lover, hus-
band, teacher. He should be able to
endure everything, should like everybody, should
love his parents, his wife, his country;
or he should not be attached to anything or any-
body, nothing should matter to him, he
should never feel hurt, and he should always be se-
rene and unruffled. He should always
enjoy life; or he should be above pleasure and en-
joyment. He should be spontaneous;
he should always control his feelings. He should
know, understand, and foresee everything.
he should be able to solve every problem of his
own, or of others, in no time. He should
be able to overcome every difficulty of his as soon
as he sees it. He should never be tired
or fall ill. He should always be able to find a job.
He should be able to do in one hour
which can only be done in two to three hours.
--Karen Horney

There are a lot of good things that have come out of psychology, but there are more than a few that are questionable. From my humble perspective, one of the most questionable notions out of pop psychology is that you *should* always feel good about yourself, that your self-esteem *should* always be high.

This notion has led to giving every child a medal or trophy at the end of a competition, no matter how well or poorly they performed. I'm all for every kid getting a *participation certificate*, but not a medal or trophy. Medals and trophies imply that you did well against your competition; sometimes, we do well against the competition and are rightly rewarded with a bronze, silver, or gold medal. On the other hand, if we finished outside the top three, I don't think we should get a medal. Instead, I believe we just need to take some satisfaction from the fact that we competed against the best and got a more realistic sense of where we stand.

All this may sound harsh to you. I don't believe it is. I think we live in a world that has made self-esteem something you don't ever mess with. I believe we are not helping people by saying that everyone's self-esteem should be high. Your sense of *worth* is supposed to be high and unchanging, given that you are a fearfully and wonderfully made human being. Your sense of *self-esteem* needs to be based on how good or bad you are at a given endeavor in life.

Let me use *American Idol*™ to drive home what I'm saying. When people audition for the show, I would want each of them to have a high sense of their *worth* as a human being, regardless of whether they make the cut to go further. But, if they can't carry a tune in a bucket and sing in a manner that makes dogs bark, I don't want them to have high self-esteem as a singer. Having high self-esteem as a singer would be completely unwarranted if you sing in a way that makes people's ears bleed.

My family only allows me to sing when I'm by myself, in my car, and the stereo turned up really, really loud. Personally, I believe I sound like a male Celine Dion; apparently, my family doesn't share that belief. What I need to do is keep my sense of worth separate from how well or poorly I sing; I need an accurate sense of my competence as a singer to have reality-based self-esteem in that area.

If it turns out my family is right—something highly suspect, given that I think they are jealous of my world-class voice—then I need to adjust my self-esteem as a singer to a level that is commensurate with my abilities. If my family is right, I will need to have a high sense of worth as a person, but low self-esteem as a singer.

You might be wondering why I'm making such a big deal about the difference between worth and self-esteem. The main reason is that people with an *overly high sense of self-esteem* are often the ones causing the most trouble and doing the most damage to the world we live in. Let me explain.

Narcissists are among the most destructive people on the planet. Three of the deadliest features of being narcissistic are: having a grandiose sense of self-importance; exaggerating one's achievement and talent; and expecting to be recognized as superior, without really being superior. Back to my earlier example, narcissism would have me being grandiose enough to think I really do sing like the male Celine Dion and wanting to be recognized as such when, in reality, I break glass with the sound of my voice. If I were to act out on my false grandiosity about my singing voice, I would find as many people as I could to support me in getting a recording contract and becoming famous, taking them down with me in the process. Anyone who supported this effort on my part would be throwing their time and money down the drain, and not thinking too well of themselves or me when everything fell apart.

Go back to childhood for a minute. What I'm talking about is why it is so deadly to overly praise a kid in order to build up their self-esteem. I've seen far too many "helicopter parents" tell their kids how awesome they did on the baseball field when the kid booted every ground ball in sight, couldn't get their bat anywhere near a pitch, couldn't find the strike zone with a map or a flashlight, and got picked off first base twice after being walked.

What a parent needs to avoid in those situations is telling their kid, "You were awesome today!" Saying that to a kid who can't walk and chew gum at the same time overly inflates their sense of self as an athlete and as a kid. This sets the stage for a lot of heartbreak down the road when they don't make the baseball or softball team in high school, much less college.

What you do say to your kid in that situation is, "I'm so proud of how hard you tried out there today. We'll keep working on hitting, fielding, and throwing so we can find out how good you are at this sport. But, know this, how you did today has absolutely nothing to do with your worth as a human being—that is something you came with being fearfully and wonderfully made."

Yea, I know, you're not going to say all of that to your kid when they walk off the baseball or soccer field, but I'd like you to say something like that, rather than blow smoke in your kid's ear by telling him or her they were awesome and are going to play professional sports someday.

Now, let's go back to you and me. What I want for all of us as adults is that we have a constant, stable sense of worth, but, at the same time, I want us to be humble enough to have an accurate sense of self-esteem regarding how good or bad we are at things like being married, raising kids, doing our jobs, and enjoying hobbies. Never let your sense of worth fluctuate based on your performance in these or any areas of life, but please let your self-esteem fluctuate about how you perform.

Don't buy into the pop psychology notion that your self-esteem should always be high. That's a crazy notion, something to be avoided like the plague. Go out there and try anything you like, but don't think more or less highly about your level of self-esteem than your performance warrants.

Chapter 22

What Should Have Happened Did

*When something happens, the only thing in
your power is your attitude toward it. It is not
the things that disturb us, but our interpretation
of their significance. Things and people are not
what we wish them to be nor are they what they
seem to be. They are what they are.*
—Epictetus

Normally, I close out a book with guidance on how to take what you've learned and put it into action. I've saved all that for the workbook. (You have been doing the workbook, haven't you?). In this, our last chapter, I want you to be a lay philosopher and grapple with one of the most important truths available to us while we're on the planet: What should have happened did.

That statement may sound like a falsehood to some of you. To others, it may sound like a script for being fatalistic in life and passively accepting whatever comes your way. To others, it may sound like pop psyche drivel compelling you to put a false smile on your face about the painful things that come your way. It is none of the above.

"What should have happened did" can free you from shoulding all over yourself with shame and con-

96

demnation when things don't go your way. Let me tell you how.

Let's go back to an example I used in the first chapter: "I shouldn't have missed my exit." Think about what you're saying. What your saying is that you're having a hard time accepting the fact that you missed your exit. Why? Because, in an ideal world, you wouldn't have missed your exit.

The only problem is that, in the real world, you should have missed your exit because you were five lanes over and not paying attention to what you were doing. How could you have possibly made your exit when you did everything necessary to miss it? In that moment, the more surprising thing would have been for you to make your exit, given that you were five lanes over and not paying a lick of attention.

Let's try another example: "I shouldn't have been late to the meeting." Again, in an ideal world, you wouldn't have been late to the meeting because in an ideal world you're never late to anything. The only problem is, you don't live in an ideal world right now and, because you weren't managing your time well, you should have been late for the meeting and you were. The more surprising thing would have been if you had gotten to your meeting on time, given that you weren't managing your time properly.

Let's try another example: "I shouldn't have yelled at my kids for being rowdy." In an ideal world, parents never yell at their kids because parents have perfect control over their thoughts, feelings, and actions. In the real world, we don't come anywhere close to that, so we end up yelling at our kids when they get on our last nerve.

I'm not saying it's right; I'm just saying most of us are this way. Since you are an imperfect human being when it comes to having perfect self-control, you're going to yell at your kids sometimes; you just need to apologize, ask for forgiveness, and try to stop yelling at them.

Let's shift to when we should all over others. When you say, "That guy shouldn't be riding my bumper," you're referring to an ideal world where no one rides your bumper. You don't get to drive in that world, much less live in it. You live in the real world where people do that kind of thing. Some people are not paying attention, or are being narcissistic, or are in an emergency situation, and they are going to ride your bumper whether you like it or not. What would be more surprising is if people like that don't ride your bumper.

Let's try another example: "My boss shouldn't be such a royal pain to work for." When you say that to yourself, you're referring to an ideal world where every boss is a wonderful, competent human being. Again, you don't get to live in that world. You live in the real world, where some bosses are not-so-wonderful, incompetent human beings who are a royal pain in the arse to work for. Some bosses are not nice or competent; they should be a pain to work for and are.

Let's try still another: "My spouse shouldn't be so hard to get along with." Since your spouse is a deadly combination of selfish, lazy, and immature, as are all of us, how could he or she not be hard to get along with? Those three bad qualities help make up our fallen inclination; those qualities are what make it hard to get along with every ("every" includes us) spouse at times.

I'm trying to get you to see that when it comes to what happens in the real world (as opposed to the ideal world in your mind), "What should have happened did." I'm not telling you to like everything that happens to you, or to do nothing about what happens to you. I don't want you to like that you missed your exit, your kids are being rowdy, or someone is riding your bumper. I just don't want you to stiff-arm what happened just because it doesn't comport with how you ideally think life should be. Shoulding all over the things you don't like in life is a sure prescription for being resentful and bitter, not anything you would wish on your worst enemy.

Let me walk you through how to perceive things from a, "What should have happened did" perspective the next time you encounter something difficult or bad. I'm not trying to swamp you with too much information here; I'm simply trying to drive home how important this issue is.

Some years ago, I started noticing that I needed to go to the bathroom fairly often. My initial mental reaction was, "I shouldn't need to go the bathroom this often," but I did nothing about it and didn't bother to check out what was going on.

For almost a year, I kept having the same problem. I couldn't go anywhere without needing to visit the restroom a number of times, something that was especially frustrating when I would go see a movie. I got pretty good at timing my visit to the restroom during the most boring and inconsequential time in a film so that I didn't miss much.

In the back of my mind, I knew this was a possible symptom of prostate issues, but I kept burying my head in the sand; I kept telling myself that I shouldn't be going through this and the problem should go away on its own. Despite my Dad having prostate cancer before he passed away, I kept telling myself my condition would go away.

This kept happening until my wife and kids laid down the law with me. They all said, in no uncertain terms, that I had to see my doctor and find out what was going on. In an adamant yet loving way, they said If I didn't see my doctor, they would shoot me and bury me in the backyard.

I finally saw my doctor, and he ordered a PSA (Prostate-Specific Antigen) screening test to assess the problem. If your PSA score falls in the 0 to 4 range, you're safe. If it falls in the 4 to 6 range, it's "safe for most." If it falls in the 4 to 10 range, it's "suspicious." And, if it's 10 or above, it's "dangerous" and you probably have prostate cancer. My score was 11.4. That made my doctor fall out of his doctor chair and my family breakdown in tears.

I had unwisely thrown away a year of my life, shoulding all over the issue of needing to go to the bathroom so much. Although I can't prove it, I think if I had gone to see my doctor earlier, the cancer wouldn't have gotten so bad.

Because I had stiff-armed reality for so long, nine of the twelve sections they biopsied of my prostate had cancer on them. Now, it wasn't a matter of, "Am I going to do anything about this?" but, "What am I going to do about this?"

I decided to go the surgery route and have my prostate removed. Doing that is no guarantee you'll be cancer-free, but it was what I felt led to do. I thank God, my family, and modern medicine that since my surgery my PSA score has been stable at 0.

I'm not trying to gross you out about my frequent need to go to the bathroom or about needing surgery to address prostate cancer. I'm simply trying to tell you that you can risk losing your life if you stiff-arm reality by saying it shouldn't be the way it is, and by refusing to do something about it.

In light of the fact my Dad had prostate cancer, I have a fallen body, there are over 190,000 new cases of prostate cancer a year, and 1 in 9 men are going to be diagnosed with prostate cancer, what should have happened did when it came to me having it.

I'm glad I finally listened to my family, because I sure have enjoyed the 16 or so years since I was diagnosed with prostate cancer. If I had kept shoulding all over my medical issues and refused to do anything about them, I wouldn't have gotten to see all three of my children get married, reach the 40-year mark in my marriage, written additional self-help books (including this one), been able to travel the world, develop closer friendships, or been able to bounce three of the most precious grandchildren in the world on my knee.

Our shoulds can literally cost us our lives. If they don't cost us our physical lives, they certainly can cost us our emotional and relational lives by eating away at them like the cancer they are. The shame and condemnation we experience, the bitterness and resentment we feel, and the sense of victimization we have in life, are all trying to tell us something. They are trying to tell us we are shoulding all over ourselves and others and it has to stop. If we want to be emotionally and relationally cancer-free and live life fully and richly, the shoulding has to stop.

I'll be praying for you. I'll be praying that you become more aware of your shoulds, accept that you have them, have compassion that they are making your life more difficult and painful than it already is, and overcome them in the months and years to come. Don't get discouraged in your efforts to do so. The journey from condemnation to compassion is a long and difficult one that has a lot of stops and starts, but it is certainly worth it.

Stop Shoulding All Over Yourself Workbook

A Comprehensive Program
for Overcoming Your
Shoulds

Chris Thurman Ph.D.

CONTENTS

Lesson 1	Assessing Your Shoulds	107
Lesson 2	I Shouldn't Make Mistakes	112
Lesson 3	I Should Be Able to Get More Done	118
Lesson 4	I Should Be Able to Control My Circumstances	125
Lesson 5	I Should Know More Than I Do	131
Lesson 6	I Should Be Happier Than I Am	137
Lesson 7	I Shouldn't Do Embarrassing Things	143
Lesson 8	I Shouldn't Be Addicted to Anything	149
Lesson 9	I Should Be More Sensitive to Others	154
Lesson 10	I Shouldn't Forget Things	160
Lesson 11	I Should Be More Successful	165
Lesson 12	I Should Like Everything About the Way I look	172
Lesson 13	I Should Be Emotionally Smarter	179
Lesson 14	I Should Be in a Better Mood	186
Lesson 15	I Should Know What I Want to Do with My Life	193

Lesson 16   I Shouldn't Have Bad Habits   200

Lesson 17   I Shouldn't Be Losing a Step   206

Lesson 18   I Shouldn't Have a Bad Bent   212

Lesson 19   I Should Be a Better Commu-   220
             nicator

Lesson 20   I Shouldn't Have Unlikeable   225
             Qualities

Lesson 21   I Should Have High Self-   232
             Esteem

Lesson 22   What Should Have Happened,   239
             Did

Lesson 1

Assessing Your Shoulds

Awareness of our shoulds and shouldn'ts is a big step in the right direction of overcoming these toxic and destructive ways of thinking.

Complete the self-assessment inventory using the scale below. Be honest in terms of how you actually think and avoid responding in terms of how you "should" think. Also, try to avoid using the neutral response (4).

1	2	3	4	5	6	7
Strongly Disagree			Neutral		Strongly Agree	

_____   1. I shouldn't make mistakes.

_____   2. I should be able to get a lot more done.

_____   3. I should be able to control my circumstances.

_____   4. I should know a lot more than I do.

_____   5. I should be a lot happier than I am.

_____   6. I shouldn't do embarrassing things.

_____ 7. I shouldn't be addicted to anything.

_____ 8. I should be more sensitive to others.

_____ 9. I shouldn't forget things.

_____ 10. I should be a lot more successful.

_____ 11. I should like everything about the way I look.

_____ 12. I should be emotionally smarter.

_____ 13. I should be in a much better mood.

_____ 14. I should know what I want to do with my life.

_____ 15. I shouldn't have any bad habits.

_____ 16. I shouldn't be losing a step.

_____ 17. I shouldn't have a bad bent.

_____ 18. I should be a much better communicator.

_____ 19. I shouldn't have any unlikeable qualities.

_____ 20. I should have high self-esteem.

Add all your responses and divide by 20. This is the average degree to which you agree or disagree with these should statements. Next, look through your answers and circle the statements you gave 5, 6, or 7. These responses suggest that you hold more strongly to these particular shoulds/shouldn'ts. Finally, look at the statements you gave 6 or 7. These are the should/shouldn't statements you struggle with the most and the ones you might want to pay special attention to in the future.

For the next seven days, be on the lookout for when you find yourself falling into shame or condemnation. Write down what event triggered those feelings and which of the twenty shoulds/shouldn'ts listed above played into you feeling that way.

The event I felt shame and condemnation about:

_____

_____

_____

_____

The shoulds that tripped me up:

_____

_____

_____

_____

The event I felt shame and condemnation about:

_____

_____

_____

_____

The shoulds that tripped me up:

_____

_____

_____

_____

The event I felt shame and condemnation about:

_____

_____

_____

_____

The shoulds that tripped me up:

_____

_____

_____

_____

Awareness is half the battle when it comes to overcoming your shoulds. By filling out the self-assessment, you're more aware of the specific should and shouldn'ts that you believe most strongly. By identifying when you feel shame and condemnation and looking for the should that was underneath feeling that way, you will be more aware of the link between the two.

See you in the next lesson.

Recommended Reading:
Get Out of Your Mind and Into Your Life: The New Acceptance and Commitment Therapy by Steven C. Hayes

Self-Compassion: The Proven Power of Being Kind to Yourself
    by Kristin Neff
*The Mindful Self-Compassion Workbook: A Proven Way to
    Accept Yourself, Build Inner Strength, and Thrive* by
    Kristin Neff and Christopher Germer.

Lesson 2

I Shouldn't Make Mistakes

In this lesson, we're going to go after the fact that we beat ourselves up for being human and making mistakes. I want you to spend this week zeroing in on your tendency to should all over yourself for making mistakes.

In the space provided, write down any mistakes you make this week, no matter how small, and what kind of shaming and condemning thoughts you had about making each mistake.

Mistake #1:

_____

_____

_____

_____

Shaming and Condemning Thoughts:

_____

_____

_____

_____

Mistake #2:

_____

_____

_____

_____

Shaming and Condemning Thoughts:

_____

_____

_____

_____

Mistake #3:

_____

_____

_____

Shaming and Condemning Thoughts:

_____

_____

_____

_____

Now, go back to each mistake you made and make the argument, "What should have happened did," given what was going on with you in the moment, and the flaws and defects you bring into day-to-day situations.

Why what should have happened, did when I made Mistake #1:

_____

_____

_____

_____

_____

_____

Why ~~w~~hat should have happened, did when I made Mistake #2:

_____

_____

_____

_____

_____

_____

_____

Why what should have happened, did when I made Mistake #3:

_____

_____

_____

_____

_____

_____

_____

Next, write down what you learned from making the mistake you made and how you can correct it next time you're in a similar situation.

What I learned from making Mistake #1 and how I can correct it next time:

_____

_____

_____

_____

_____

_____

_____

_____

What I learned from making Mistake #2 and how I can correct it next time:

_____

_____

_____

_____

_____

_____

_____

What I learned from making Mistake #3 and how I can correct it next time:

_____

_____

_____

_____

_____

_____

_____

Finally, I want you to write a brief essay entitled, "Since I Am Finite and Flawed, I Should Make a Lot of Mistakes Along the Way."

_____

_____

_____

_____

_____

_____

_____

_____

_____

_____

_____

_____

_____

_____

_____

_____

_____

_____

The purpose of this lesson is to get you to quit shaming and condemning yourself for being a human being who makes a lot of mistakes. It is to convince you to accept the fact that you are anything but perfect, given the flaws and defects you have, and that mistakes are going to be common in your day-to-day life. Finally, it is to get you to have more compassion and grace toward yourself each day, so when you make mistakes, instead of becoming shaming and condemning, you treat yourself kindly and empathically.

Because we are going to make a lot of mistakes as we go through life, we need to get off our own backs, accept the mistakes we made, have compassion that we made the mistakes, and focus all of our energy on simply correcting the mistakes and moving on. Easier said than done, but very much worth doing.

Recommended Reading:

I Thought It Was Just Me (but it isn't) by Brene Brown

The CBT Workbook for Perfectionism by Sharon Martin

The Gifts of Imperfection: Let Go of Who You Think You Should Be and Accept Who You Are by Brene Brown

Lesson 3

I Should Be Able to Get More Done

We all want to be productive. When it comes to productivity, we can make one of two major mistakes. One is to expect to get more done than a finite human being can do. The other is to not get as much done as we were capable of doing.

Let's start with expecting yourself to get more done than a human being can do. In the spaces provided below, write down the areas of your life where you find yourself expecting to get more done than you can.

I expect to get more done than I can when it comes to

_____

_____

_____

_____

I expect to get more done than I can when it comes to

_____

_____

_____

_____

I expect to get more done that I can when it comes to

_____

_____

_____

_____

Next, turn your attention to areas of your life where you don't get enough done. Without beating yourself up, write down some examples of when you haven't gotten as much done as you actually had the time and ability to do.

I haven't gotten as much done as I could have when it comes to

_____

_____

_____

_____

I haven't gotten as much done as I could have when it comes to

_____

_____

_____

_____

I haven't gotten as much done as I could have when it comes to

_____

_____

_____

_____

In areas of your life where you expect too much of yourself, what can you do to set more realistic goals? For example, let's say you're working on finishing a writing project. The more realistic goal, given that you have many areas of life to contend with, might be to have the goal of writing for thirty minutes a day.

A more realistic goal when it comes to

_____

_____

_____

_____

would be

_____

_____

_____

_____

A more realistic goal when it comes to

_____

_____

_____

_____

would be

_____

_____

_____

_____

A more realistic goal when it comes to

_____

_____

_____

_____

would be

_____

_____

_____

_____

In areas of your life where you aren't getting enough done, what do you need to do to make sure you step it up a little and get more accomplished? For example, let's say you aren't getting enough things done around the house. What might you do to address that (ask a friend to hold you accountable for addressing one thing a day; set aside time every day to work on doing these things; not allowing yourself to do something enjoyable until you have done the harder things first, etc.)?

I could get more of

_____

_____

_____

accomplished if I commit to

_____

_____

_____

_____

I could get more of

_____

_____

_____

accomplished if I commit to

_____

_____

_____

_____

_____

I could get more of

_____

_____

_____

accomplished if I commit to

_____

_____

_____

_____

_____

Finally, because you can only be in one place at a time, doing one thing at a time, I want you to write a brief essay, "When I'm Working Hard and Being Focused, I Shouldn't Get Anymore Done Than I'm Getting Done."

_____

_____

_____

_____

_____
_____
_____
_____
_____
_____
_____
_____
_____
_____
_____
_____
_____
_____
_____
_____
_____
_____
_____

The purpose of this lesson is to get you to compassionately accept your limitations when it comes to how much you can do in a given day, while pushing you to not give into lethargy or laziness when it comes to getting things done. It's a tough tightrope to walk, but a really important one, because we are supposed to "produce the goods" in our personal and professional lives. Let's not overreach or underreach when we are trying to accomplish things each day.

Recommended Reading:

Having a Mary Heart in a Martha World: Finding Intimacy with God in the Busyness of Life by Joanna Weaver

Margin: Restoring Emotional, Physical, Financial, and Time Reserves to Overloaded Lives by Richard Swenson

The Ruthless Elimination of Hurry: How to Stay Emotionally Healthy and Spiritually Alive in the Chaos of the Modern World by John Mark Comer

Lesson 4

I Should Be Able to Control My Circumstances

It's hard to accept that we have very little control over external circumstances while we're here. So much of what happens to us in life is beyond our control, and that is unsettling because events can occur that significantly impact how our lives turn out.

The first thing I want you to do is write down what you're trying to control in life but can't. For example, you have no control over whether or not you get a promotion at work, only over the quality of your work and how hard you're working.

I have no control over

_____

_____

_____

_____

_____

even though I'm trying to control it/him/her.

I have no control over

_____

_____

_____

_____

_____

even though I'm trying to control it/him/her.

I have no control over

_____

_____

_____

_____

_____

even though I'm trying to control it/him/her.

I have no control over

_____

_____

_____

_____

_____

even though I'm trying to control it/him/her.

I have no control over

_____

_____

_____

_____

_____

even though I'm trying to control it/him/her.

The next thing I want you to do is write down areas of your life where you have influence but aren't exercising the influence you have. For example, you have some degree of influence over your children by practicing what you preach and disciplining them when they are out of line but are not doing either.

I have influence over

_____

_____

_____

but I'm not exercising the influence I have because

_____

_____

_____

_____

I have influence over

_____

_____

_____

but I'm not exercising the influence I have because

_____

_____

_____

_____

I have influence over

_____

_____

_____

but I'm not exercising the influence I have because

_____

_____

_____

_____

Next, without beating yourself up, I want you to write down areas of your life where you are not exercising control over your own thoughts, feelings and actions. For example, you might struggle to control toxic "self-talk" in how you mentally react to things that trigger you, struggle to rein in your emotions when reacting to things you find aversive, and control your actions when you get "dysregulated" about painful situations.

I struggle to control

_____

_____

_____

when aversive things happen to me.

I struggle to control

_____

_____

_____

when aversive things happen to me.

I struggle to control

_____

_____

_____

when aversive things happen to me

Next, I want you to zero in on one specific area of your life you are trying to control that you have no control over, and how you are unhealthily trying to control it:

_____

_____

_____

_____

_____

_____

_____

Now, turn your attention to one area of your life that you can control (eating, spending, working, etc.) and what it would take for you to exert more self-control in that area (join a compulsive eating, spending, working 12-Step program and join with others who struggle with the same thing):

_____

_____

_____

_____

_____

_____

_____

_____

Finally, given that we don't have unlimited power in life and other people have free will, I want you to write a brief essay, "I Shouldn't Be Able to Control Things Outside of Me but Can Control More of What's Going on Inside of Me."

_____

_____

_____

_____

_____

_____

_____

_____

_____

_____

_____

_____

_____

_____

_____

_____

_____

The purpose of this lesson is to help you stop trying to control the things you can't, start trying to influence things to the degree you can, start having more self-control over the toxic thoughts, feelings and actions that are causing you harm, and bathe all of it in compassion and grace. It is crucial, as we go through life, to accept what we can't control, try to influence what we can, and develop greater self-control over our thoughts, feelings, and actions.

Recommended Reading:

Codependent Not More: How to Stop Controlling Others and Start Caring for Yourself by Melody Beattie

The Control Freak: Coping with Those Around You, Dealing with the One Within by Les Parrott

Lesson 5

I Should Know More Than I Do

We often get down on ourselves because of how little we know while we're here, rather than accepting how much there is to know and how limited we are in our capacity to know it.

First, I want you to write down when you fell into shaming and condemning yourself for something you didn't know.

I got down on myself because I didn't know

_____

_____

_____

_____

I got down on myself because I didn't know

_____

_____

_____

_____

I got down on myself because I didn't know

_____

_____

_____

_____

Second, I want you to zero in on your specific area of expertise in life and guess what percentage you know of all the things that can be known in that area:

_____

Third, across the areas listed below, guess how much you know of all that can be known in those areas (I'm giving you a long line to write on because you're going to need a lot of decimal points):

_____ Physics

_____ Chemistry

_____ Biology

_____ Mathematics

_____ History

_____ Economics

_____ Philosophy

_____ Foreign Languages

_____ English Literature

_____ Theology

_____ Engineering

_____ Astronomy

_____ Health

_____ Art

_____ Music

_____ Physical Science

_____ Geography

_____	Psychology
_____	Sociology
_____	Anthropology
_____	500 Other Subject Matters

Fourth, I want you to guess what percentage you know of all that can be known (you're going to need even more decimal points for this one):

_____

_____

_____

Fifth, without beating up yourself or others, write down some of the reasons you don't know as much as you could about various subject matters (keep in mind things like laziness, it was more enjoyable to party, only have twenty-four hours in a day, aren't a genius, poor-quality teaching, inadequate access to knowledge, getting married and having kids, being exhausted, mental overload, etc.):

A. _____

_____

B. _____

_____

C. _____

_____

D. _____

_____

E. _____

_____

Sixth, what personal or professional price have you paid for not knowing more than you do in various areas of life (don't rub your nose in it, just assess the damage not knowing more has caused to your life)?

_____

_____

_____

_____

_____

_____

_____

_____

_____

Seventh, what subject matters would you like to learn more about and what practical step are you willing to take to learn more about them?

I'd like to learn more about _____

_____

and I could do _____

_____

to learn more about it.

I'd like to learn more about _____

_____

and I could do _____

_____

to learn more about it.

I'd like to learn more about _____

_____

and I could do _____

_____

to learn more about it.

Eighth, what class are you willing to take, book are you willing to read, Netflix™ show are you willing to watch, or YouTube™ video are you willing to watch to learn something new each week?

A. _____

_____

B. _____

_____

C. _____

_____

Finally, given how much there is to know, I want you to write a short essay, "Given How Much There is to Know and How Finite I Am, I Should Only Know an Infinitesimally Small Part of All that Can Be Known."

_____

_____

_____

_____

_____

_____

_____

_____
_____
_____
_____
_____
_____
_____
_____
_____
_____
_____
_____
_____
_____
_____
_____
_____

The purpose of this lesson is to help you more graciously accept how little you know as you go through life, without lazily settling for not learning enough. We can always learn more, and that's why we need to have good study habits. Whether it's in our area of professional expertise or in areas of study we find interesting and want to learn more about, we all need to burn more of the midnight oil.

Recommended Reading:

Humility: The Journey Toward Holiness by Andrew Murray

Humility: True Greatness by C.J. Mahaney

Lesson 6

Should Be Happier Than I Am

It's normal to want to be happy as we go through life. Unfortunately, some of us think that we should be "walking on sunshine" happy all the time, something that is not the least bit realistic in a world like ours.

I'm reminded of a song by the Byrds from the 1960's, *Turn, Turn, Turn*©. Drawing from the book of Ecclesiastes, the song was about there being "a time to laugh, a time to weep," and "a time to dance, a time to mourn." There is a time for the pleasant emotions, and there is a time for the painful ones.

Not to start off on a negative note, I want you to write down the things you have done to "make yourself happy" that were unwise or misguided. For example, you might have tried to make yourself happy by buying something you couldn't afford or eating 12 glazed donuts. Think through the last few years and write down things that you did to make yourself happy that only caused you more unhappiness.

I tried to make myself happy by

_____

_____

_____

_____

and all it did was cause me more unhappiness in the form of

_____

_____

_____

_____

I tried to make myself happy by

_____

_____

_____

_____

and all it did was cause me more unhappiness in the form of

_____

_____

_____

_____

I tried to make myself happy by

_____

_____

_____

_____

and all it did was cause me more unhappiness in the form of

_____

_____

_____

_____

Obviously, when we try to make ourselves happy in ways that only make us more unhappy, we need to chart a new path.

Now, think through the ways you have tried to make yourself feel happy that were good for you and left you better off. For example, you may have tried to make yourself happy by listening to music, learning something new, or getting into a healthy exercise routine, and those activities left you feeling happier. Looking back over the last few years, write down what you did that was good for you and made you feel happy.

I tried to make myself happy by

_____

_____

_____

_____

and it left me better off by

_____

_____

_____

_____

I tried to make myself happy by

_____

_____

_____

_____

and it left me better off by

_____

_____

_____

_____

I tried to make myself happy by

_____

_____

_____

_____

and it left me better off by

_____

_____

_____

_____

Obviously, we want to do a lot more of these kinds of things. I'm no happiness expert, but one of the keys to being a happier person is to do the things that are healthy in and of themselves, and that leave you adding value to your life in some meaningful way.

It's essay time. Given that wanting to feel happy all the time is delusional, write an essay entitled, "I Shouldn't Feel Happy All the Time, but I Don't Want to Make a Habit of Feeling Unhappy and Can Do Healthy Things to Be a Happier Person."

_____

_____

_____

_____

_____

_____

_____

_____

_____

_____

_____

_____

_____

_____

_____

_____

_____

_____

_____

_____

_____

The purpose of this lesson is to help you accept the fact that you are supposed to experience both pleasant and painful emotions in life, to stop shoulding all over yourself when you're not happy, to stop trying to make yourself feel happy in unhealthy ways, and to get into the habit of doing healthy, meaningful activities that can help you feel happy. In the midst of it all, I want you to have compassion for yourself that there is a season for painful emotions in life and not be down on yourself about it.

I leave you with a quote by Henry David Thoreau, "I am a happy camper so I guess I'm doing something right. Happiness is like a butterfly; the more you chase it, the more it will elude you, but if you turn your attention to other things, it will come and sit softly on your shoulder."

Recommended Reading:

The Happiness Advantage: How a Positive Brain Fuels Success in Work and Life by Shawn Achor

The Happiness Trap: How to Stop Struggling and Start Living
by Russ Harris

Stumbling on Happiness by Daniel Gilbert

Switch on Your Brain: The Key to Peak Happiness, Thinking, and Health by Caroline Leaf

Lesson 7

I Shouldn't Do Embarrassing Things

Doing embarrassing things is a part of life. It is an inescapable sign that we don't always have our thinking cap on when we take action. While it's certainly not pleasant, we all experience some humiliating "fails" in life, things that we wish no one saw.

Take a minute to write down your "Top Five Most Embarrassing Fails." Obviously, I don't want you to beat yourself up about something that happened in your past, so please don't do that as you conjure these things up. Describe what you did, who was there to see it, and rate on a 0-100 scale how embarrassed you felt.

Most Embarrassing Fail #1:

_____

_____

_____

_____

_____

_____

_____

_____

_____

_____

_____

Most Embarrassing Fail #2:

_____

_____

_____

_____

_____

_____

_____

_____

_____

_____

Most Embarrassing Fail #3:

_____

_____

_____

_____

_____

_____

_____

_____

_____

_____

Most Embarrassing Fail #4:

_____

_____

_____

_____

_____
_____
_____
_____
_____
_____
_____

Most Embarrassing Fail #5:

_____
_____
_____
_____
_____
_____
_____
_____
_____
_____

Now, in light of the fact that "What Should Have Happened Did," go back through each fail and write down how all the planets were aligned for you to do exactly what you did. For example, I walked around a grocery store once with my fly down. I can sit there all I want and say, "I shouldn't have been walking around with my fly down," but the truth of the matter is that my fly should have been down given that I forgot to zip it up after using the restroom in the grocery store. In other words, what should have happened did. Now, your turn.

Embarrassing Fail #1 Should Have Happened Because:

_____
_____
_____
_____
_____
_____
_____
_____

Embarrassing Fail #2 Should Have Happened Because:

_____
_____
_____
_____
_____
_____
_____
_____

Embarrassing Fail #3 Should Have Happened Because:

_____
_____
_____
_____
_____
_____

_____

_____

Embarrassing Fail #4 Should Have Happened Because:

_____

_____

_____

_____

_____

_____

_____

_____

Embarrassing Fail #5 Should Have Happened Because:

_____

_____

_____

_____

_____

_____

_____

_____

The purpose of this lesson is to get you to stop shoulding all over yourself that you do embarrassing things, have compassion toward yourself that these kinds of things are going to happen at times, take a closer look at why they happen so that we don't do them again, and learn to laugh at ourselves about it. In other words, I want you to get off your own back when it comes to the fact that your humanness sometimes shows up in ways that are embarrassing and humbly join the human race.

Recommended Reading/Viewing:

Embarrassing Moments on Live TV—YouTube
Most Embarrassing & Funny Moments in Sports—YouTube
So Embarrassing: Awkward Moments and How to Get Through Them by Charise Mericle Harper
Supermarket Fails/Epic Supermarket Fails—YouTube

Lesson 8

I Shouldn't Be Addicted to Anything

Psychiatrist Gerald May is right when he said, "To be alive is to be addicted." We are wired to move in the direction of what feels good in life and move away from what feels bad. When doing something makes us feel better, we are more likely to turn to it again and again. Ultimately, if we aren't careful, we become addicted and are in bondage to certain things for how we're coping with life, much to our own demise.

Take a few minutes to put a check mark by any of the following things you are addicted to. As the joke goes, "Denial is not a river in Egypt," so try not to deny that you are addicted to anything listed below if the truth of the matter is you are.

_____ television	_____ exercise	_____ Caffeine
_____ Food	_____ Shipping	_____ Gaming
_____ Drugs	_____ Work	_____ Internet
_____ love	_____ Plastic surgery	_____ Lying
_____ Risky behavior	_____ Music	_____ Piercing
_____ tattoos	_____ sugar	_____ tanning
_____ lip balm	_____ chewing ice	_____ water
_____ social media	_____ rejection	_____ hoarding

_____	sniffing fumes	_____	vaping	_____	approval
_____	anime	_____	applause	_____	cannabis
_____	stubbornness	_____	drama	_____	diuretics
_____	isolating	_____	joking	_____	Junk
_____	lust	_____	laziness	_____	MSG
_____	prayer	_____	pornography	_____	chocolate
_____	Religion	_____	smoking	_____	sleeping
_____	therapy	_____	self-help	_____	therapy
_____	travel	_____	wealth	_____	nervous tics
_____	codependency	_____	fantasizing	_____	fame
_____	energy drink	_____	perfectionism		

To be alive is to be addicted, and I don't want you shoulding all over yourself that this painful reality happens to be true of you. The thing with addictions is that they are best dealt with in a group setting working through a twelve-step program. With that in mind, I want you to look back at what you checked above. If you checked a number of things, zero in on one or two that you would like to put your time and energy overcoming in the months and years to come. Then, figure out what program would be best for you to become a part of so that your efforts can be supported properly.

The addiction I want to work on is

_____

_____

and the way I'm going to work on it is

_____

_____

_____

What I want to push you on in this lesson is to have compassion for yourself that you are addicted to many things. I want you to have compassion for yourself because the addictions you are caught up in have been extremely costly to you and those who love you. In others words, you have been inflicting a great deal of unnecessary suffering on your life and the lives of others because of your addiction, making your life and theirs much harder than they had to be. Instead of shaming and condemning yourself about this, I want you to have empathy and compassion for yourself and those around you who have been so negatively impacted by your addictions. In the space below, write a letter of contrition and compassion to yourself and others for how your addictions have been self-destructive.

_____

_____

_____

_____

_____

_____

_____

_____

_____

_____

_____

_____

_____

_____

_____

_____

_____

_____

_____

_____

_____

_____

_____

Please, stop shaming and condemning yourself that your addicted to many things while you're here. Keep trying to accept that you have these addictions and bathe them in compassion and kindness that they have made your life a lot harder than it had to be. Acceptance of your addictions and compassion about having them are the necessary precursors to getting some help and staying the course in overcoming them.

Finally, as we have done with each should or shouldn't, I want you to write a brief essay, "Given That to Be Alive is to Be Addicted, I Should Have Ended Up Addicted to the People, Places, and Things That I'm Addicted to in Life but Will Chart a New Course."

_____

_____

_____

_____

_____

_____

_____

_____

_____

_____

_____

_____

_____

_____

_____

_____

_____

_____

_____

_____

The purpose of this lesson is to get you to face what you're addicted to, have compassion that you're addicted to it, and channel your energy in the direction of doing something about it. Please, stop denying that you're addicted, have compassion that certain things have you by the throat and are choking you to death, and join with other addicted human beings to break free so that your life can be what it was meant to be.

Recommended Reading:

Addiction and Grace by Gerald May
Addictions: A Banquet in the Grave by Ed Welch
Unbroken Brain: A Revolutionary New Way of Understanding Addiction by Maia Szalavitz

Lesson 9

I Should Be More Sensitive to Others

Because we all lack empathy to some degree, we are all prone to be insensitive to how our actions impact other people. We are all prone to be *narcissistic* in that we focus too much on ourselves and lack compassion and sensitivity for how our actions affect those around us.

Without rubbing your face in it, take a minute to think about the ways you have been insensitive to others in terms of how your actions have been hurtful to them. Be specific as to what you did, the person you hurt, how they felt in the midst of your actions, and whether or not you have made amends to them by apologizing and changing your behavior.

I have been hurtful to

_____

by_____

_____

_____.

Walking around in their shoes, they must have felt

_____

_____

_____

_____

_____

given how I was acting. What I have done to correct my
hurtful behavior is

_____

_____

_____

_____

_____

I have been hurtful to

_____

by_____

_____

_____.

Walking around in their shoes, they must have felt

_____

_____

_____

_____

_____

given how I was acting. What I have done to correct my
hurtful behavior is

_____

_____

_____

_____

I have been hurtful to

_____

_____

by_____

_____.

Walking around in their shoes, they must have felt

_____

_____

_____

_____

_____

given how I was acting. What I have done to correct my hurtful behavior is

_____

_____

_____

_____

I have been hurtful to

_____

_____

by_____

_____.

Walking around in their shoes, they must have felt

_____

_____

_____

_____

_____

given how I was acting. What I have done to correct my hurtful behavior is

_____

_____

_____

_____

I have been hurtful to

_____

_____

by_____

_____

_____.

Walking around in their shoes, they must have felt

_____

_____

_____

_____

_____

given how I was acting. What I have done to correct my hurtful behavior is

_____

_____

_____

_____

The issue in life isn't "Am I going to be hurtful and insensitive to others?" That's a given in light of our natural bent toward narcissism. The issue is "Do I really care that I've been hurtful and insensitive to others, and have I made amends by apologizing and correcting my actions?" The most damaging people on the planet are the ones who *don't care* that their actions are hurtful to others. Their narcissism is so toxic that they cause harm everywhere they go and never repair the damage they cause. Avoid them at all costs.

Given that we are all narcissistic to some degree (have a grandiose sense of self-importance, preoccupied with fantasies of unlimited success and brilliance, believe that we are special and unique, require excessive admiration, have a sense of entitlement, interpersonally exploitative, lack empathy for the feelings and needs of others, envious of others or believe they are envious of us, and show arrogant and haughty attitudes and behavior), write an essay entitled "I'm Going to Be Insensitive at Times to Others but Need to Have Empathy for Their Pain and Repair the Damage I've Caused."

_____

_____

_____

_____

_____

_____

_____

_____

_____

_____

_____

_____

_____

_____

_____

_____

_____

_____

_____

_____

_____

_____

The purpose of this lesson is to get you to face the fact that being grandiose and self-absorbed is going to lead to being hurtful to others and that you need to have more empathy for how your actions impact those you love. We all need to have more empathy toward those around us in terms of how our actions cause hurt to the souls of others. Without beating ourselves up, we need to correct the wrong actions we engage in, have empathy for the pain others are in who are on the receiving end of our hurtful actions, confess our wrongdoings to them, ask for forgiveness, and make amends by changing our actions for the better.

Recommended Reading:

Crucial Conversations: Tools for Talking When the Stakes Are High by Kerry Patterson, Joseph Grenny, Ron McMillan, and Al Switzler

Hold Me Tight: Seven Conversations for a Lifetime of Love by Sue Johnson

Just Listen: Discover the Secret of Getting Through to Absolutely Anyone by Mark Goulston

The War for Kindness: Building Empathy in a Fractured World by Jamil Zaki

Lesson 10

I Shouldn't Forget Things

I don't pretend to understand all the issues that come into play for why we forget things. I just know that we do and that we need to stop beating ourselves up about it. Not only is it true that "To err is human," but it is equally true that "To forget is human," and shaming and condemning ourselves about it only makes it worse.

First, I want you to write down the kinds of things you tend to forget. Be specific as to what you forget, who is impacted by your forgetting, and how they are impacted. Let me lead by example:

I tend to forget people's names, it seems to have the biggest impact on people I know at church, and the impact it seems to have on some of them is feeling like they are not important enough for me to remember their name.

I tend to forget people's birthday's, it seems to have the biggest impact on the friends whose birthdays I forget, and the impact it seems to have on some of them is that they are not important enough for me to remember their birthday.

I tend to forget

_____

_____

it seems to have the biggest impact on

_____

and the impact it has on them is

160

_____

_____

_____

I tend to forget

_____

_____

it seems to have the biggest impact on

_____

and the impact it has on them is

_____

_____

_____

I tend to forget

_____

_____

it seems to have the biggest impact on

_____

and the impact it has on them is

_____

_____

_____

I tend to forget

_____

_____

it seems to have the biggest impact on

_____

and the impact it has on them is

_____

_____

_____

I tend to forget

_____

_____

it seems to have the biggest impact on

_____

and the impact it has on them is

_____

_____

Second, I want you to strategize as to how you might do a better job of remembering things. I'm not up on all the phone and computer apps available, but it's my understanding that there are apps that can help you remember things that might get by you if you leave it up to your own devices for remembering appointments, birthdays, anniversaries, people's names, facts, and others things of importance. I would encourage you *not* to depend too much on other people to remind you about things—it's a royal pain for most of them to do given their tendency to forget, plus, as we say here in Texas, they didn't take you to raise.

_____

_____ will help me remember

_____ better.

_____
_____ will help me remember
_____ better.

_____
_____ will help me remember
_____ better.

_____
_____ will help me remember
_____ better.

_____
_____ will help me remember
_____ better.

Finally, because none of us has a perfect memory, I want you to write another "What Should Have Happened Did" essay entitled, "I Should Forget Things Given That I'm Human and Can Do a Number of Things to Get Better at Remembering."

_____
_____
_____
_____
_____
_____
_____
_____
_____
_____
_____

_____

_____

_____

_____

_____

_____

_____

_____

_____

_____

_____

_____

The purpose of this lesson is to help you accept the fact that you are going to forget things, to have compassion toward yourself and others that you do, and to put guardrails in place that can help serve as your memory for you. "To forget is human," but we don't need to be indifferent to that fact or overly indulge it.

Recommended Reading:

Keeping Love Alive as Memories Fade: The Five Love Languages and the Alzheimer's Journey by Gary Chapman

Memory Rescue: Supercharge Your Brain, Reverse Memory Loss, and Remember What Matters Most by Daniel Amen

Practical Memory: A Practical Guide to Remember More & Forget Less in Your Everyday Life by I.C. Robledo

Lesson 11

I Should Be More Successful

You may not have struggled with this particular "should" in your life. Whether you struggle with this one very much, I want you to spend some time working on it.

First, I want you to write down the areas of life that you either felt you should have been a huge success at or more successful than you have been. And, don't worry about how "small" the area of life is. For example, it's okay to say, "I should have been more of a success at organizing my time" or "I should have been more of a success at cleaning out my garage."

I should have been more of a success at

_____

_____

_____

I should have been more of a success at

_____

_____

_____

I should have been more of a success at

_____

_____

_____

I should have been more of a success at

_____

_____

_____

I should have been more of a success at

_____

_____

_____

Now that you've figured out where you "should have" been more of a success at certain things, I want you to go back through each one and write down the reasons you weren't more successful at it.

I'm not providing you with a bunch of *excuses*, but think about choosing from among the following *reasons* why you weren't more successful at certain things: 1) didn't have the ability to do it better; 2) didn't have the time to do it better; 3) didn't have the money to do it better; 4) didn't have the training to do it better; 5) didn't have the emotional support to do it better; 6) didn't have the internal motivation to do it better (even though I still should all over myself about it); 7) circumstances that were beyond my control got in the way of me doing it better; 8) others got in the way of me being more successful at it; 9) I copped out and threw a half-baked effort at it even though I had all the time, money, and support I needed; and 10) other life events were more important to focus on.

I wasn't more of a success at

_____

_____

because

_____

_____

_____

_____

I wasn't more of a success at

_____

_____

because

_____

_____

_____

_____

I wasn't more of a success at

_____

_____

because

_____

_____

_____

_____

I wasn't more of a success at

_____

_____

because

_____

_____

_____

I wasn't more of a success at

_____

_____

because

_____

_____

_____

_____

Now, zero in on *one* area of life where you would like to be more successful and write down what you need to do to achieve it. Go back to the ten reasons we *aren't* more successful at things and turn them around to your advantage. Choose an area to be more successful at in which: 1) you have the ability to get better; 2) you have the time to get better at it; 3) you have the money to get better at it; 4) you have training/instruction available to you for being more successful at it; 5) you have the emotional support you need from others to get better at it; 6) you are sufficiently motivated to get better at it; 7) there are no major external circumstances blocking you; 8) there is nobody significantly blocking your efforts; 9) you are going to give it your all; and 10) there aren't any life events that are more important for you to attend to.

The area of my life I'm going to try to be more success-ful at is

_____

_____

_____and I have checked all the appropriate boxes for getting it done:

_____ have the ability to get better at it;

_____ have the time to get better at it and that time is from _____ to _____ on this day of the week _____.

_____ have the money to get better at it and have set aside this amount _____.

_____ have accessed the training/instruction I need and am going to get it from _____ at this time each week:

_____ have asked _____ _____ to give me emotional support along the way;

_____ am sufficiently motivated to not only start this effort but to finish it;

_____ there are no significant externals circumstances getting in my way;

_____ there is no individual or group of individuals getting in the way;

_____ I'm going to give it my all;

_____ I'm not putting getting better at this ahead of more important things that need my time, talents, and treasures.

If you can't check all ten boxes, I would encourage you to look for something else to get better at. You don't want to shoot yourself in the foot by trying to be more successful at something that is doomed to fail from the start because you didn't have the ability, time, money, training, emotional support, motivation, external circumstances, people circumstances, effort level, and priorities all in their proper place.

Not to beat it to death, but I want you to write a brief essay entitled, "I Shouldn't Be Any More Successful Than I Am Given All the Things That Affect Success, But I Can Do More to Be Successful in the Future."

_____

_____

_____

_____

_____

_____

_____

_____

_____

_____

_____

_____

_____

_____

_____

The purpose of this lesson is to get you to stop shoulding all over yourself about the fact that you haven't been as successful at certain things as you would like, have compassion for yourself about it, see what's been getting in the way of being more successful, clear those barriers out of the way, and go achieve more of your realistic dreams in life. None of us want to live with regrets when it comes to not doing what it takes to be more successful in life.

Recommended Reading:

Grit: The Power of Passion and Perseverance by Angela Duckworth

The 7 Habits of Highly Effective People: Powerful Lessons in Personal Change by Stephen Covey

The Road Less Traveled: A New Psychology of Love, Traditional Values and Spiritual Growth by M. Scott Peck

Thinking Fast and Slow by Daniel Kahneman

Lesson 12

I Should Like Everything About the Way I Look

You gotta feel for the blob fish, turkey vulture, warthog, proboscis monkey, star-nosed mole, and matamata turtle, don't you? They always make the "Top Ten Ugliest Animals" list. God bless the blob fish, he/she takes the number one spot every time.

In a world obsessed with looks, a lot of us walk around feeling like the blob fish about our appearance, shaming and condemning ourselves along the way. Here, I want to challenge you to stop shoulding all over yourself that you have a feature or two (or twenty) that isn't looked all that highly upon in our shallow, looks-obsessed world.

Take a minute to thing about any aspect of your physical appearance that you don't like. Write it down in the spaces provided below.

When it comes to my physical appearance, I don't like

_____

_____

_____

When it comes to my physical appearance, I don't like

_____

_____
_____

When it comes to my physical appearance, I don't like

_____
_____
_____

When it comes to my physical appearance, I don't like

_____
_____
_____

When it comes to my physical appearance, I don't like

_____
_____
_____

Now, think through each physical feature you don't like and decide which category to put it in.

Physical Feature I Don't Like #1:

_____
_____
_____

_____ I can't do anything about it and need to just accept it as it is

_____ I can do something about it but am going to just accept it as it is

173

_____ I'm going to do something about it as soon as I have the time and money to do so

_____ Whether I can do anything about it or not, I'm going to not only accept it as it is but celebrate it because it gives me some degree of uniqueness as a human being

_____ This is all nonsense, and I'm going to continue not to pay it much attention

Physical Feature I Don't Like #2:

_____

_____

_____

_____ I can't do anything about it and need to just accept it as it is

_____ I can do something about it but am going to just accept it as it is

_____ I'm going to do something about it as soon as I have the time and money to do so

_____ Whether I can do anything about it or not, I'm going to not only accept it as it is but celebrate it because it gives me some degree of uniqueness as a human being

_____ This is all nonsense, and I'm going to continue not to pay it much attention

Physical Feature I Don't Like #3:

_____

_____

_____

_____ I can't do anything about it and need to just accept it as it is

_____ I can do something about it but am going to just accept it as it is

_____ I'm going to do something about it as soon as I have the time and money to do so

_____ Whether I can do anything about it or not, I'm going to not only accept it as it is but celebrate it because it gives me some degree of uniqueness as a human being

_____ This is all nonsense, and I'm going to continue not to pay it much attention

Physical Feature I Don't Like #4:

_____

_____

_____

_____ I can't do anything about it and need to just accept it as it is

_____ I can do something about it but am going to just accept it as it is

_____ I'm going to do something about it as soon as I have the time and money to do so

_____ Whether I can do anything about it or not, I'm going to not only accept it as it is but celebrate it because it gives me some degree of uniqueness as a human being

_____ This is all nonsense, and I'm going to continue not to pay it much attention

Physical Feature I Don't Like #5:

_____

_____

_____

_____ I can't do anything about it and need to just accept it as it is

_____ I can do something about it but am going to just accept it as it is

_____ I'm going to do something about it as soon as I have the time and money to do so

_____ Whether I can do anything about it or not, I'm going to not only accept it as it is but celebrate it because it gives me some degree of uniqueness as a human being

_____ This is all nonsense, and I'm going to continue not to pay it much attention

Finally, write an essay entitled, "I Shouldn't Like Everything About the Way I Look Given That Not Everything About the Way I Look is Attractive (In the World's Shallow Eyes), but It's Okay to Want to Improve a Few Things as Long as It Isn't to Make Myself Feel More Worthwhile or Loveable."

_____
_____
_____
_____
_____
_____
_____
_____
_____
_____
_____

_____

_____

_____

_____

_____

_____

_____

_____

_____

_____

_____

The purpose of this lesson is to get you to accept everything about how you look whether or not it is attractive in the world's eyes, have more compassion about the physical qualities you have that the world tends to look down on, improve your appearance however you think best, but do so within the constraints of wanting to do it rather than feeling like if you don't that you are not a worthwhile or loveable human being. Beauty is only skin deep, and those that have a beautiful exterior by worldly standards are fortunate (although, it can also be a curse). Internal beauty is the kind of beauty to pay more attention to. The side benefit to internal beauty is that it makes you more externally beautiful. Work on internal beauty, and you win twice.

Recommended Reading:

The Body Image Workbook: An Eight-Week Program for Learning to Like Your Looks by Thomas Cash

Chris Thurman, Ph.D.

Compared to Who? A Proven Path to Improve Your Body Image
by Heather Creekmore
*Feeling Good About the Way You Look: A Program for Over-
coming Body Image Problems* by Sabine Wilhelm

Lesson 13

I Should Be Emotionally Smarter

We all lack relational smarts. To be human is to be relationally lacking in intelligence when it comes to knowing yourself well and knowing how to interact with others in a sophisticated manner.

The main qualities of emotional intelligence are self-awareness (knowing and understanding yourself), self-regulation (being able to control your impulses and stay calm in the face of upsetting situations), empathy (being aware of and considerate toward the feelings of others), motivated (being internally motivated and able to motivate others), and social skills (pulling all these qualities together in a nice package when interacting with others). As you can tell, developing your emotional intelligence is no easy task, but it is something that we need to do to be healthier and more effective when interacting with others.

Spend this week focusing on emotional intelligence by being more aware of when you feel sad, angry, hurt, anxious, guilty, and happy. In the spaces provided below, write down when you felt each of these emotions and what event triggered them.

I felt sad this week when:

_____

_____

_____

179

_____

_____

_____

_____

_____

_____

I felt angry this week when:

_____

_____

_____

_____

_____

_____

_____

_____

I felt hurt this week when:

_____

_____

_____

_____

_____

_____

_____

_____

I felt anxious this week when:

_____

_____

_____
_____
_____
_____
_____
_____
_____

I felt guilty this week when:

_____
_____
_____
_____
_____
_____
_____
_____

I felt happy this week when:

_____
_____
_____
_____
_____
_____
_____
_____

Sadness is triggered by loss, anger is triggered by blocked goals, hurt is triggered by unmet psychological needs, anxiety is triggered by threat, guilt is triggered by doing something wrong, and happiness is triggered by pleasurable things going your way. Go back to each of these emotions that you listed above and write out what triggered them.

When I felt sad, the loss I experienced was

_____

_____

_____

_____

_____

_____

_____

_____

_____

When I felt angry, the blocked goal I experienced was

_____

_____

_____

_____

_____

_____

_____

_____

When I felt hurt, the unmet psychological needs (attention, acceptance, appreciation, affirmation, affection, comfort, encouragement, respect, security, support, and understanding) I experienced were

_____
_____
_____
_____
_____
_____
_____
_____
_____

When I felt anxious, the threat I experienced was

_____
_____
_____
_____
_____
_____
_____
_____

When I felt guilty, the wrong thing I did was

_____
_____
_____
_____
_____
_____
_____
_____

When I felt happy, the pleasurable things that went my way were

_____

_____

_____

_____

_____

_____

_____

_____

In light of the fact that what should have happened did, I want you to write a brief essay entitled "I Shouldn't Be an Emotional Genius Given That No One Ever Showed Me How or Modeled It for Me, but I Can Become More Emotionally Intelligent If I Work at It."

_____

_____

_____

_____

_____

_____

_____

_____

_____

_____

_____

_____

_____

_____

_____

_____

_____

_____

_____

_____

_____

The purpose of this lesson is to help you stop shoulding all over yourself that you lack emotional intelligence to some degree, have compassion toward yourself that no one showed you how and you're having to learn it now as an adult, and do what you can to learn how to be an emotionally intelligent human being. We're all left-footed when it comes to interacting with others in an emotionally intelligent manner, let's just keep working on trying to raise our "E.Q" so that we get better at it over time.

Recommended Reading:

Emotional Intelligence: Why It Can Matter More Than IQ by Daniel Goleman

Emotional Intelligence 2.0 by Travis Bradberry and Jean Greaves

Permission to Feel: Unlocking the Power of Emotions to Help Our Kids, Ourselves, and Our Society Thrive by Marc Brackett

The Whole Brain Child: 12 Revolutionary Strategies to Nurture Your Child's Developing Mind by Daniel Siegel

Lesson 14

I Should Be in a Better Mood

Bad (painful) moods are a normal part of life. The healthy goal is to not have them too frequently, stay in them too long, or allow them to be so intense that we can't function all that well.

As we explored in the last lesson on emotional intelligence, it is important to be more aware of what you're feeling and what event triggered your emotional response. To put this differently, given that we experience upsetting events in life, we should be in a bad (painful) mood at times. Let's go back into what triggers painful emotions so that we can stop shoulding all over ourselves when we are in a bad mood.

Sadness is the painful emotion we feel when we have experienced a loss of some kind (death of a loved one, loss of a job, loss of self-esteem because we messed something up, etc.). Think back to the last few times you were sad. What was the loss you experienced?

I felt sad when

_____

_____

and the loss involved was

_____

_____

_____

I felt sad when

_____

_____ and the loss involved was_____

_____

_____

_____

I felt sad when

_____

_____ and the loss involved was_____

_____

_____

Anger is the painful emotion we feel when something blocks or frustrates a goal we have (trying to get across town and you run into a traffic jam, you're trying to communicate and someone keeps interrupting you, etc.). Think back to the last few times you were angry. What was the blocked goal you experienced?

I felt angry when

_____

_____ and the blocked goal involved was

_____

_____

I felt angry when

_____

_____ and the blocked goal involved was

_____

_____

Chris Thurman, Ph.D.

I felt angry when

_____

_____ and the blocked goal involved was

_____

_____

Anxiety is the painful emotion we feel when something poses a threat to us (someone is walking toward us with a knife and a menacing look, you hear about a round of layoffs coming at work, you've lost your job and don't know how you are going to pay your bills, etc.). Think back to the last time you felt anxious. What was the physical or psychological threat involved?

I felt anxious when

_____

_____ and the threat involved was

_____

_____

I felt anxious when

_____

_____ and the threat involved was

_____

_____

I felt anxious when

_____

_____ and the threat involved was

_____

_____

Hurt is the painful emotion we feel when valid psychological needs go unmet (respect, appreciation, support, understanding, attention, affirmation, encouragement, acceptance, security, affection, and comfort). Think back to the last time you felt hurt. What was the unmet psychological need involved?

I felt hurt when

_____

_____

_____ and the unmet psychological need involved was

_____

_____

I felt hurt when

_____

_____

_____ and the unmet psychological need involved was

_____

_____

_____

I felt hurt when

_____

_____

_____ and the unmet psychological need involved was

_____

_____

_____

Guilt is the painful emotion we feel when we have done something wrong (lied, stole, cheated, betrayed someone, overindulged, etc.). Think back to the last time you felt guilty. What was the wrong thing you did?

I felt guilt when

_____

_____

_____and the wrong thing I did was

_____

_____

I felt guilt when

_____

_____

_____ and the wrong thing I did was

_____

_____

I felt guilt when

_____

_____

_____ and the wrong thing I did was

_____

_____

Feeling sad, angry, anxious, hurt, and guilty are all a normal part of how we are supposed react to the things that happen that "put us in a bad mood." Again, this is normal, and we just have to be careful not to let our bad mood get too intense, last too long, or show up too frequently.

When we're in a bad mood, we need to avoid falling into destructive coping (alcohol and drug use, yelling at people, isolating, etc.) and try to cope in a constructive manner (talk it over with someone, pray, exercise, meditate, engage in rational self-talk, reach out to others that are hurting to help them, experience nature, etc.). What are some of the best ways you can cope with a bad mood so that you don't make it worse.

I can constructively cope with a bad mood by

_____

_____

_____

_____

I can constructively cope with a bad mood by

_____

_____

_____

_____

I can constructively cope with a bad mood by

_____

_____

_____

_____

In light of the fact that painful emotions and the bad mood that goes along with them are a normal part of life, write a brief essay entitled, "I Should Be in a Bad Mood at Times, and Here Are Some Healthy Things I Can Do About It."

_____

_____

_____

_____

_____

_____

_____

_____

_____

_____

_____

_____

_____

_____

_____

_____

The purpose of this lesson is to get you to accept that painful emotions are a normal part of life, have compassion for yourself that these painful emotions bang around in our soul, and deal with them in the most healthy and constructive way possible. Bad moods are coming our way, we just need to be ready for them so that they move on through like bad weather.

Recommended Reading:

The Feeling Good Handbook by David Burns

Get Out of Your Mind and Into Your Life: The New Acceptance and Commitment Therapy by Steven C. Hayes

Mind Over Mood: Change How You Feel by Changing the Way You Think by Dennis Greenberger and Christine Padesky

Lesson 15

I Should Know What I Want to Do with My Life

More than a few of us struggle with feeling like how we're wired in terms of our interests, abilities, and passions isn't a very good match for the job we do. When that's the case, it can be hard to drag ourselves out of bed each morning as we head off to work. It certainly doesn't help to beat ourselves up that we don't have this figured out yet.

Figuring out what we want to be when we grow up is no easy task. I'm going to leave that up to others for helping you with that. There are a lot of good occupational/vocational counselors who might be able to help you find a line of work that lights your fire. If you think going that route would be helpful, I would encourage you to ask around to see whose name comes up for being able to support you finding a good fit.

In this lesson, I'm going to assume that you are staying in your current position for a while and try to encourage you when it comes to how to make the job you're in more enjoyable. In doing so, I'm asking you to put aside "I should have all this figured out by now" and simply accept the fact that you don't, have compassion toward yourself about it, and do the best you can to make your current job more pleasant and meaningful.

If you're in that unenviable position of not knowing what to do with your life and not being happy in the job you have, try these twelve tips on for size when it comes to making what you do more enjoyable. In the space provided, write down how you could implement these tips into your job life.

Challenge Yourself by Adding a New or Extra Assignment:

_____
_____
_____
_____
_____
_____
_____
_____
_____

Ask for Help from Your Boss or a Co-Worker for How to Do Your Job Better:

_____
_____
_____
_____
_____
_____
_____
_____
_____

Find Balance (do more fun things, spend time with friends, work out, take breaks):

_____
_____

_____

_____

_____

_____

_____

_____

_____

Do an Outside of Work Passion Project:

_____

_____

_____

_____

_____

_____

_____

_____

_____

Do Kind Things for Co-Workers:

_____

_____

_____

_____

_____

_____

_____

_____

_____

Get to Know People Better at Work While Avoiding Overly Intimate Conversations:

_____
_____
_____
_____
_____
_____
_____
_____
_____

Reward Yourself for a Job Well Done:

_____
_____
_____
_____
_____
_____
_____
_____

Go Outside for a Break:

_____
_____
_____
_____
_____
_____
_____
_____

Change Things You Don't Like (if you can):

_____
_____
_____
_____
_____
_____
_____
_____
_____
_____

Leave Work at the Office:

_____
_____
_____
_____
_____
_____
_____
_____
_____

Smile More Often:

_____
_____
_____
_____
_____
_____
_____

_____

_____

_____

Solve a Situation/Make a Helpful Suggestion:

_____

_____

_____

_____

_____

_____

_____

_____

In light of the fact that it can be hard to match who you are with a job that lights your fire, do whatever you can to make your current job more enjoyable until you go in a new direction. Don't let a bad attitude about your job spill over into the job itself. Every job, no matter how much or little you may like it, is a blessing and to be appreciated.

In light of "What should have happened did," write a brief essay entitled, "I Still Haven't Found What I'm Looking for in a Job, But I'm Going to Make the One I'm In as Enjoyable as Humanly Possible."

_____

_____

_____

_____

_____

_____
_____
_____
_____
_____
_____
_____
_____
_____
_____
_____
_____
_____
_____

The purpose of this lesson is not to help you find a job that melts your butter but to get you to stop shoulding all over yourself if you haven't and turn your current job into a more enjoyable experience. Have compassion for yourself that you haven't been able to find a great job just yet, be happier in the job you have, and keep looking for something better to come along in the future.

Recommended Reading:

It's Your Attitude: Out with the Bad, In with the Good by
    Chris Thurman
Man's Search for Meaning by Viktor E. Frankl
The Purpose-Driven Life by Rick Warren
*What Color is Your Parachute 2020: A Practical Manual for
    Job-Hunters and Career Changers* by Richard N.
    Bolles

Lesson 16

I Shouldn't Have Bad Habits

Everyone has bad habits. The challenge is to replace them with good habits so that when we are stressed out or anxious, we cope with things in a healthier manner.

What are your bad habits? In the space provided below and without beating yourself up for it, write them down. Make sure you distinguish between an addiction (alcohol) and a bad habit (interrupting people) in what you write down.

Bad Habit #1:

_____

_____

Bad Habit #2:

_____

_____

Bad Habit #3:

_____

_____

Bad Habit #4:

_____

_____

Bad Habit #5:

_____

_____

What is underneath your bad habits? Think about what you are trying to cope with when you fall into these habits.

With Bad Habit #1, I'm usually coping with:

_____

_____

With Bad Habit #2, I'm usually coping with:

_____

_____

With Bad Habit #3, I'm usually coping with:

_____

_____

With Bad Habit #4, I'm usually coping with:

_____

_____

With Bad Habit #5, I'm usually coping with:

_____

_____

What are some good habits that you might try to replace some of your bad habits with, ways of coping with emotional pain that leave you better off?

Good Habit #1:

_____

_____

Good Habit #2:

_____

_____

Good Habit #3:

_____

_____

Good Habit #4:

_____

_____

Good Habit #5:

_____

_____

New habits are hard to develop and take persever-ance. How are you going to persevere in the face of de-veloping the good habits you mentioned above?

How I'm Going to Persevere to Develop Good Habit #1:

_____

_____

_____

_____

_____

How I'm Going to Persevere to Develop Good Habit #2:

_____

_____

_____

_____

_____

_____

How I'm Going to Persevere to Develop Good Habit #3:

_____

_____

_____

_____

_____

_____

How I'm Going to Persevere to Develop Good Habit #4:

_____

_____

_____

_____

_____

_____

How I'm Going to Persevere to Develop Good Habit #5:

_____

_____

_____

_____

_____

_____

Given that we are all prone to develop bad habits along the way, I want you to write a short essay entitled, "I Should Have Bad Habits, but I Can Replace Them with Good Habits If I Try Hard Enough."

_____

_____

_____

_____

_____

_____

_____

_____

_____

_____

_____

_____

_____

_____

_____

_____

_____

_____

The purpose of this lesson is to encourage you to move away from shoulding all over yourself that you have bad habits and to extend grace and compassion to yourself about it. And, it is to challenge you to do what you can to replace your bad habits with good ones. Never forget to extend compassion to yourself when you're trying to overcome your shoulds and shouldn'ts.

Recommended Reading:

Atomic Habits: An Easy & Proven Way to Build Good Habits & Break Bad Ones by James Clear

The Power of Habit: Why We Do What We Do in Life and Business by Charles Duhigg

The 7 Habits of Highly Effective People by Stephen R. Covey

Tiny Habits: The Small Changes That Change Everything by BJ Fogg

Lesson 17

I Shouldn't Be Losing a Step

Everyone loses a step (or two or twenty) as they get older. It's inevitable. The issue here is whether or not we are going to grow old gracefully or go down kicking and screaming like a petulant five-year-old. Far too many of us choose the latter.

One of my favorite movies is *On Golden Pond*. It's a beautifully done film, the acting, writing, and directing are all fantastic. *On Golden Pond* is about a couple, Norman and Ethel Thayer, who are in their sunset years. Ethel has grown old gracefully and is kind to everyone. Norman, on the other hand, has grown old not-so-gracefully and walks around in a grumpy huff all the time. The thing Norman is especially having a hard time accepting is the fact that he has gotten older and has lost some degree of the mental and physical sharpness he used to have when he was younger.

My wife, Holly, is Ethel, and I'm Norman. As my wife gets older, she is even more kind, gracious, and supportive. As I get older, I get ornerier and more cantankerous. Pray for Holly if you will. Like Norman, I'm always carping about something, and Holly, like Ethel, responds with empathy and understanding as she tries to help her husband do something constructive about what he's griping about.

Take a few minutes to write down how you are losing a step in life (physically, emotionally, and spiritually) and how you've reacted to it (Ethel or Norman?). Don't beat yourself up about it, just own it. And, just because your hair hasn't turned gray yet, you're not off the hook. Even if you're in your twenties or thirties and are full of vim and vigor, you're losing a step or two in some way.

Example #1 of How I'm Losing a Step and My Reaction to It:

_____

_____

_____

_____

Example #2 of How I'm Losing a Step and My Reaction to It:

_____

_____

_____

_____

Example #3 of How I'm Losing a Step and My Reaction to It:

_____

_____

_____

_____

Example #4 of How I'm Losing a Step and My Reaction to It:

_____

_____

_____

_____

Example #5 of How I'm Losing a Step and My Reaction to It:

_____

_____

_____

_____

Next, put a check mark by any of the things listed below that you do, all of which make you age faster.

_____ Don't get enough sleep

_____ Smoke

_____ Crash diet

_____ Drink too much

_____ Skip fruits and vegetables

_____ Hold on to grudges

_____ Too much of a couch potato

_____ Carry around stress

_____ Lack of friendships

_____ Lack of exercise

_____ Bad eating habits

_____ Don't get out enough

_____ Not drinking enough water

_____ Don't learn anything new

In light of these kinds of things being what makes you lose a step faster, what can you do to slow this trend in your life?

To Slow the Pace of Losing a Step, I Can:

_____

_____

_____

_____

To Slow the Pace of Losing a Step, I Can:

_____

_____

_____

_____

To Slow the Pace of Losing a Step, I Can:

_____

_____

_____

_____

To Slow the Pace of Losing a Step, I Can:

_____

_____

_____

_____

To Slow the Pace of Losing a Step, I Can:

_____

_____

_____

_____

Write a brief essay, "Given That I'm Getting Older, I Should Be Losing a Step, but I Can Do the Following Healthy Things About It."

_____

_____

_____

_____

_____

_____

_____

_____

_____

_____

_____

_____

_____

_____

_____

_____

_____

_____

_____

_____

As with every other lesson in this workbook, I'm trying to get you to stop shoulding all over yourself about being a human being, humbly accept the limitations you bring into the world each day, have compassion about it being pretty rough out there, and passionately commit to staying on the path of growth and development before your life is all said and done. We're all losing a step as we get older, and we don't want to self-destructively speed that process up by not doing the things we can do to live healthier lives of greater passion and meaning.

Recommended Reading:

The Gift of Years: Growing Older Gracefully by Joan Chittiser

On the Brink of Everything: Grace, Gravity, and Getting Old by Parker J. Palmer

Successful Aging: A Neuroscientist Explores the Power and Potential of Our Lives by Daniel J. Levitin

Lesson 18

I Shouldn't Have a Bad Bent

Whether we want to admit it or not, every human being has a fallen bent. While we all have worth, none of us are "good" in the sense that we are naturally loving and moral in how we think, feel, and act each day.

As always, I don't want you to rub your own face in this, but I do want to challenge you to face this painful truth about having a bent in the direction of the bad and see what you can do about it. With that in mind, let me take you into the three main ways you have a bad bent.

One aspect of having a bad bent is that you are bent in the direction of being selfish rather than selfless. In other words, you are prone to take rather than give, think about yourself rather than others, and want to be at the head of the line rather than let others go first. Without shaming yourself, what are some of the most selfish things you have done during your life?

One of the most selfish things I have ever done is:

_____

_____

_____

_____

_____

One of the most selfish things I have ever done is:

_____

_____

_____

_____

_____

One of the most selfish things I have ever done is:

_____

_____

_____

_____

_____

Another aspect of having a fallen bent is that you are prone to being lazy rather than hard-working. This has to do with the pleasure principle, the dynamic that we don't like pain and are drawn in the direction of pleasure. Hard work is painful, so we don't naturally like doing it. Without condemning yourself, what are some of the laziest things you have done in your life?

One of the laziest things I have ever done is:

_____

_____

_____

_____

_____

One of the laziest things I have ever done is:

_____

_____

_____
_____
_____

One of the laziest things I have ever done is:

_____
_____
_____
_____
_____

Finally, another way you have a fallen bent is that you have a tendency to react like a five-year-old when people don't meet your needs or hurt you in some way. Rather than respond in a healthy, assertive manner to interpersonal wounds, we often respond by pulling away, attacking, being passive-aggressive, self-medicating, and/or trying harder to get others to treat us better. None of that ever helps and usually makes things worse. Without beating yourself up, what are some of the most immature ways you have responded to people not giving you what you want or mistreating you?

One of the most immature ways I reacted to feeling angry and hurt toward others is:

_____
_____
_____
_____
_____

One of the most immature ways I reacted to feeling angry and hurt toward others is:

_____

_____

_____

_____

_____

One of the most immature ways I reacted to feeling angry and hurt toward others is:

_____

_____

_____

_____

_____

In light of our fallen bent toward selfishness, laziness, and immaturity, write down how you could work on improving in those areas.

One way I could be more *selfless and giving* is to:

_____

_____

_____

_____

_____

One way I could be more *selfless and giving* is to:

_____

_____

_____

_____

_____

_____

One way I could be more *selfless and giving* is to:

_____

_____

_____

_____

_____

One way I could me more *hard-working* in life is:

_____

_____

_____

_____

_____

One way I could me more *hard-working* in life is:

_____

_____

_____

_____

_____

One way I could me more *hard-working* in life is:

_____

_____

_____

_____

_____

One way I could respond more *maturely* when I feel hurt and angry toward others is:

_____

_____

_____

_____

_____

One way I could respond more *maturely* when I feel hurt and angry toward others is:

_____

_____

_____

_____

_____

One way I could respond more *maturely* when I feel hurt and angry toward others is:

_____

_____

_____

_____

_____

Throughout your life, you're always going to be battling your bent toward being selfish, lazy, and immature (although I must add that some people seem to have given up the fight and are living lives of chronic selfishness, laziness, and immaturity). Have compassion for yourself and others that we all struggle with this "unholy trinity" of character defects but don't have to spend the rest of our lives giving in to them.

In light of the fact that "What should have happened did," write a brief essay entitled "I Should Be Selfish, Lazy, and Immature at Times Given My Fallen Bent, but I Don't Have to Make It a Lifestyle."

_____
_____
_____
_____
_____
_____
_____
_____
_____
_____
_____
_____
_____
_____
_____
_____
_____
_____
_____
_____
_____
_____

The purpose of this lesson is to get you to quit shoulding all over yourself that you have a fallen bent, to break you out of denial about it being true, to encourage you to have compassion on yourself and others that we all struggle in these various ways, and to challenge you to stop giving in to your selfish, lazy, and immature bent and become more selfless, hard-working, and mature in how you deal with life. The path to true joy in life is paved with being a giver, working hard, and responding maturely to the things that disappoint or hurt you.

Recommended Reading:

The Freedom of Self-Forgetfulness: The Path to True Christian Joy by Tim Keller

The Giving Tree by Shel Silverstein

Humility: The Beauty of Holiness by Andrew Murray

I Like Giving: The Transforming Power of a Generous Life by Brad Formsma

Maturity: Growing Up and Going on in the Christian Life by Sinclair B. Ferguson

Lesson 19

I Should Be a Better Communicator

Very few of us know how to communicate well. I'm not putting us down; I'm simply telling it like it is. Most of us have a hard time taking what is in our mind and expressing it to others in a way that doesn't leave them scratching their heads about what in the world we are trying to say.

There are a number of communication mistakes we make and being aware that we make them is half the battle. Put a check mark alongside any of the mistakes listed below you tend to make.

_____ Speaking loudly and quickly.

_____ Bringing up the past.

_____ Defending your feelings.

_____ Judging the feelings of others.

_____ Interrupting the other person.

_____ Being overly dramatic in making your point.

_____ Blaming the other person for your feelings.

_____ Manipulatively steering the conversation in the direction you want it to go.

_____ Not maintaining eye contact.

_____ Not paraphrasing or restating what someone said to you to see if you have it right.

_____ Making assumptions about what the other person is saying.

_____ Talking too much about yourself.

_____ Not asking probing questions.

_____ Needing to win the argument.

_____ Attacking someone's character rather than addressing what they're saying.

_____ Not being empathic.

_____ Using "You" statements instead of "I" statements.

_____ Being indirect.

_____ Negative or apathetic body language.

_____ Expecting people to read your mind.

As you can see, there are a lot of ways we make mistakes when communicating to others, many more than those listed. Now that you have assessed the mistakes you make when interacting with others, choose the five that are the most damaging to your efforts to communicate and how you can turn them around.

One way I miscommunicate is by

_____

_____and I can turn that around by

_____

_____

_____
_____
_____
_____
_____

One way I miscommunicate is by

_____
_____and I can turn that around by
_____
_____
_____
_____
_____
_____

One way I miscommunicate is by

_____
_____and I can turn that around by
_____
_____
_____
_____
_____
_____

One way I miscommunicate is by

_____
_____and I can turn that around by
_____
_____

_____

_____

_____

_____

_____

One way I miscommunicate is by

_____

_____and I can turn that around by

_____

_____

_____

_____

_____

_____

Write a brief essay, "Given All the Mistakes I Make as a Communicator, I Shouldn't Be Any Better of a Communicator Than I Am, but I Can Improve My Communication Skills and Get Better at It."

_____

_____

_____

_____

_____

_____

_____

_____

_____

_____

The purpose of this lesson is to help you quit shoulding all over yourself for the communication skills you have, to encourage you to have more compassion for how hard it is to communicate well, to be more aware of the mistakes you are making when communicating to others, and to correct those mistakes as best you can. However good or bad our communication skills are, we can improve them.

Recommended Reading:

Crucial Conversations: Tools for Talking When the Stakes are High by Kerry Patterson, Joseph Grenny, Ron McMillan, and Al Switzler

How to Talk to Anyone: 92 Little Tricks for Big Success in Relationships by Leil Lowndes

Just Listen: Discover the Secret to Getting Through to Absolutely Anyone by Mark Goulston

Words That Work: It's Not What You Say, It's What People Hear by Frank Luntz

You Just Don't Understand: Men and Women in Conversation by Deborah Tannen

Lesson 20

I Shouldn't Have Unlikeable Qualities

Like it or not, we all have some unlikeable qualities. That's one reason why it is unwise of us to expect others to like everything about us.

Let's start with the positive. Look through the list of likeable qualities below and put a check mark by any that you have (at the level of "that's the way I am 51% or more of the time"). I encourage you to enjoy this list before you get to the next one. Obviously, these are the positive traits that you want to hang onto if you have them and the ones you want to develop if you don't.

_____ active	_____ adaptive	_____ affable
_____ affectionate	_____ alert	_____ ambitious
_____ attentive	_____ austere	_____ balanced
_____ benevolent	_____ careful	_____ charitable
_____ creative	_____ confident	_____ considerate
_____ compassionate	_____ considerate	_____ curious
_____ cooperative	_____ courageous	_____ diligent
_____ dependable	_____ determined	_____ dutiful
_____ disciplined	_____ dispassionate	_____ enthusiastic
_____ encouraging	_____ energetic	_____ flexible
_____ excellent	_____ faithful	_____ frugal
_____ forgiving	_____ gritty	

_____ generous	_____ gritty	_____ hardworking
_____ harmonious	_____ honest	_____ honorable
_____ hopeful	_____ humble	_____ independent
_____ industrious	_____ integrous	_____ just
_____ kind	_____ lively	_____ logical
_____ loving	_____ loyal	_____ merciful
_____ methodical	_____ mindful	_____ moderate
_____ modest	_____ neat	_____ orderly
_____ open-minded	_____ organized	_____ passionate
_____ patient	_____ persistent	_____ polite
_____ pragmatic	_____ prudent	_____ punctual
_____ purposeful	_____ rational	_____ reasonable
_____ reliable	_____ resolute	_____ respectful
_____ righteous	_____ self-disciplined	_____ sincere
_____ simple	_____ stable	_____ self-controlled
_____ steadfast	_____ strong	_____ supportive
_____ temperate	_____ thrifty	_____ tidy
_____ truthful	_____ trustworthy	_____ unselfish
_____ valiant	_____ vital	_____ warm
_____ vindictive	_____ violent	_____ volatile
_____ weak-willed	_____ whiny	_____ withdrawn
_____ workaholic	_____ worrywart	_____ welcoming
_____ witty	_____ wholesome	_____ well-spoken
_____ well-read		

Now, let's turn our attention to the downside of human personality, our unlikeable traits. Put a check mark beside any that you have (at a level of "that's the way I am 51% or more of the time"). Remember, don't beat yourself up about it, just own it. This is not an easy list to go through. When I went through it, I had no idea I had so many unlikeable qualities! Obviously, these are the qualities you want to let go of if you have them and the ones you don't want to develop ~~in~~ if you don't.

_____	Abrasive	_____	Antisocial	_____	Apathetic
_____	Callous	_____	Catty	_____	childish
_____	Cocky	_____	Compulsive	_____	Controlling
_____	Cowardly	_____	Cruel	_____	Confrontational
_____	Cynical	_____	Defensive	_____	Devious
_____	dishonest	_____	disloyal	_____	disorganized
_____	disrespectful	_____	evasive	_____	evil
_____	Extravagant	_____	fanatical	_____	Flaky
_____	Foolish	_____	Forgetful	_____	Frivolous
_____	Fussy	_____	Gossipy	_____	greedy
_____	Grumpy	_____	Gullible	_____	Haughty
_____	hostile	_____	Humorless	_____	Hypocritical
_____	ignorant	_____	impatient	_____	Impulsive
_____	Inattentive	_____	Indecisive	_____	Inflexible
_____	Inhibited	_____	Insecure	_____	Irrational
_____	Irresponsible	_____	Jealous	_____	Judgmental
_____	Know-it-all	_____	lazy	_____	macho
_____	Manipulative	_____	Materialistic	_____	Morbid

_____ mischievous	_____ Melodramatic	_____ Martyr
_____ Nagging	_____ Needy	_____ Nervous
_____ Nosy	_____ obsessive	_____ Oversensitive
_____ Paranoid	_____ Perfectionist	_____ Pessimistic
_____ Possessive	_____ Prejudice	_____ Pretentious
_____ Promiscuous	_____ Pushy	_____ Rebellious
_____ Reckless	_____ Resentful	_____ Rowdy
_____ scatterbrained	_____ Self-indulgent	_____ spoiled
_____ Selfish	_____ Sleazy	_____ superstitious
_____ Stingy	_____ stubborn	_____ Timid
_____ Suspicious	_____ tactless	_____ Ungrateful
_____ Uncouth	_____ Unethical	_____ Verbose
_____ unintelligent	_____ Vain	_____ Volatile
_____ Vindictive	_____ Violent	_____ Withdrawn
_____ Weak-willed	_____ Whiny	_____ Worrywart
_____ Workaholic		

First, a pat on the back for being willing to look through this list and own where the shoe fits. Now that you've done so, look back at all the things you've checked and pick three that you want to work on. Write down your thoughts about how you might be able to overcome these negative qualities.

I can overcome being _____ by
_____
_____
_____
_____
_____
_____
_____

I can overcome being _____ by
_____
_____
_____
_____
_____
_____
_____

I can overcome being _____ by
_____
_____
_____
_____
_____
_____
_____

Finally, write an essay entitled, "Not Everyone Should Like Everything About Me Because There are Some Things Not to Like, but I'm Going to Work on Letting Go of My Unlikeable Traits and Developing My Likeable Ones."

_____

_____

_____

_____

_____

_____

_____

_____

_____

_____

_____

_____

_____

_____

_____

_____

_____

_____

_____

_____

_____

The purpose of this lesson is to get you to stop shoulding all over yourself that you have some unlikeable traits, to have compassion for yourself that you have things about yourself that are unlikeable, to hold on to the good traits you have, and to do whatever you can to drop the bad ones.

Recommended Reading:

Mindsight: The New Science of Personal Transformation
    by Daniel J. Siegel

The Gift of Being Yourself: The Sacred Call to Self-Discovery by
    David Benner

The Road Back to You: An Enneagram Journey to Self-Discovery by Ian Cron and Suzanne Stabile

Lesson 21

I Should Have High Self-Esteem

Worth is a different matter than self-esteem. Worth is fundamentally based in being a fearfully and wonderfully made human being, not how you look, how smart you are, how much money you make, or how gifted or talented you are when it comes to the roles you have in life. You have worth the whole time you're here, whether you see it that way or not. And you will never have more or less worth anywhere along the way.

On the other hand, self-esteem, properly understood, is a function of how well or poorly you perform at the various things you attempt. If you are married but not a very loving spouse, your self-esteem as a spouse needs to be low. If you are married but are a loving and caring spouse, your self-esteem as a spouse needs to be high.

First, let's drill down into the issue of worth. Looking back on your life, what have you tended to base your worth in?

I have based my worth in

_____

_____

_____

I have based my worth in

_____

_____

_____

I have based my worth in

_____

_____

_____

I have based my worth in

_____

_____

_____

I have based my worth in

_____

_____

_____

Given that you have based your worth in the things you mentioned above, describe how your sense of worth has fluctuated, as those things have fluctuated.

_____

_____

_____

_____

_____

_____

_____

_____

Let's turn to the issue of self-esteem. Your self-esteem in a given area of life needs to be a reflection of how well or poorly you perform in that area. Without rubbing your own nose in it, what areas of your life have you had a higher sense of self-esteem than what was warranted by your performance in that area (example: I've had high self-esteem about myself as an accountant even though, truth be told, I'm not a very good accountant)?

I've had inappropriately high self-esteem in the area of_____ even though my actual performance in that area has tended to be

_____

_____

_____

_____

_____

I've had inappropriately high self-esteem in the area of_____ even though my actual performance in that area has tended to be

_____

_____

_____

_____

_____

I've had inappropriately high self-esteem in the area
of _____ even
though my actual performance in that area has tended
to be

_____

_____

_____

_____

_____

Turn this around. In what areas of your life have
you had a lower sense of self-esteem than what was
warranted by your performance in that area (example:
I've had low self-esteem as a parent even though I'm a
pretty good parent)?

I've had inappropriately low self-esteem in the area
of _____ even
though my actual performance in that area has tended
to be

_____

_____

_____

_____

_____

I've had inappropriately low self-esteem in the area
of _____ even
though my actual performance in that area has tended
to be

_____

_____

_____

_____

_____

    I've had inappropriately low self-esteem in the area of _____ even though my actual performance in that area has tended to be

_____

_____

_____

_____

_____

    Finally, let's explore where your self-esteem in certain areas of life is commensurate with your performance in that area (example: I have moderately high self-esteem as a painter that is in keeping with the fact that I'm good at it but certainly no Leonardo Da Vinci).

    My self-esteem in the area of

_____

has been commensurate with the fact that my performance in that area has been

_____

_____

_____

    My self-esteem in the area of

_____

has been commensurate with the fact that my performance in that area has been

_____

_____

_____

My self-esteem in the area of

_____

has been commensurate with the fact that my performance in that area has been

_____

_____

_____

_____

Write an essay entitled "My Worth is Permanent but
I Can Improve My Self-Esteem in the Following Ways."

_____

_____

_____

_____

_____

_____

_____

_____

_____

_____

_____

_____

_____

_____

_____

_____

_____
_____
_____
_____
_____
_____
_____
_____

Try to separate your worth from performance but humbly allow your self-esteem to be tied to how well or poorly you do the things you do. In all of this, have compassion for yourself (and others) that your sense of worth is under attack given the performance-oriented world you live in and that having accurate self-esteem is a difficult challenge as well.

Recommended Reading:

ACT Made Simple: An Easy-to-Read Primer on Acceptance and Commitment Therapy by Russ Harris

Break Free: Acceptance and Commitment Therapy in 3 Steps by Tanya Peterson

Get Out of Your Head: Stopping the Spiral of Toxic Thoughts by Jennie Allen

Get Out of Your Mind and Into Your Life: The New Acceptance and Commitment Therapy by Steven Hayes

Lesson 22

What Should Have Happened Did

O ne of the most important truths available to us in life is, "What should have happened did." What this truth acknowledges is that when you should all over yourself about something, all the factors were in play for things to happen exactly as they did. Let me give you some examples.

When you miss your exit on the highway and mentally respond by thinking, "I shouldn't have missed my exit," you're stiff-arming the reality that you should have missed your exit, given that you weren't paying enough attention. Given that you were five lanes over and texting on your cell phone, you should have missed your exit and did. What would have been shocking is if you have made your exit (without killing yourself and everyone in your path).

When you don't get as much done in a given day as you expect yourself to do, and respond by thinking, "I should have gotten a lot more done," you're stiff-arming the fact that you only had so much time and energy, ran into some unforeseen circumstances that delayed you, or gave into being lazy that day and shouldn't have gotten anymore done than you did. What would have been shocking is if you had gotten more done that day, given what you externally and internally ran into while trying to get things done.

When you do embarrassing things and respond by thinking, "I shouldn't do embarrassing things," you're

239

stiff-arming the fact that we human beings are wired to do embarrassing things and this applies to you, as well. What would have been shocking is if, at some point in your past, you had never done anything to embarrass or humiliate yourself.

Not coming to grips with the truth that "What should have happened did" shoots you like a speeding bullet into shame, condemnation, bitterness, and resentment. As if that is not bad enough, it makes it harder for you to interact with others in a healthy way. The emotional and relational damage caused by our tendency to should all over ourselves is why we need to work hard to overcome this broken part of how we view things mentally.

In the space provided below, I want you to note some recent examples of you shoulding all over yourself and write down all the "What should have happened did" thoughts that your mind can generate.

What should have happened did when I recently:

_____

_____

_____

_____

_____

_____

_____

What should have happened did when I recently:

_____

_____

_____

_____

_____

_____

_____

What should have happened did when I recently:

_____

_____

_____

_____

_____

_____

What should have happened did when I recently:

_____

_____

_____

_____

_____

_____

What should have happened did when I recently:

_____

_____

_____

_____

_____

_____

When we should all over ourselves, we are taking something which was good to *want* or *desire* and turning it into a self-condemning law or rule. For example, when I should all over myself for making a mistake, I'm taking something good, not *wanting* to make mistakes, and making it an unattainable absolute. There's nothing wrong with us not wanting to make mistakes, but there is a whole lot wrong when we turn it into a self-condemning should or shouldn't.

Go back to the deadliest shoulds/shouldn'ts you have and write out what the underlying want or desire is.

When I should all over myself about

_____

_____

_____

the underlying want or desire I have is:

_____

_____

_____

_____

When I should all over myself about

_____

_____

_____

the underlying want or desire I have is:

_____

_____

_____

_____

_____

When I should all over myself about

_____

_____

_____

the underlying want or desire I have is:

_____

_____

_____

_____

The challenge here is to stop taking healthy wants and desires and turning them into unhealthy shoulds or shouldn'ts. Take a minute to write down as long a list as you can of healthy wants or desires you have. I'll give you a little bit of a head start.

It's healthy to want to avoid making mistakes, even though I know I'm going to make them.

It's healthy to want to avoid doing embarrassing things, even though I'm going to do them.

It's healthy to want to be happier than I am, even though I know unhappiness is a part of life.

It's healthy to want:

_____

_____

_____

_____

_____

It's healthy to want:

_____

_____

_____

_____

_____

It's healthy to want:

_____

_____

_____

_____

_____

It's healthy to want:

_____

_____

_____

_____

_____

It's healthy to want:

_____

_____

_____

_____

_____

It's healthy to want:

_____

_____

_____

_____

_____

Write an essay entitled "What Should Have Hap-pened Did Given All the Factors in Play at the Time."

_____

_____

_____

_____

_____

_____

_____

_____

_____

_____

_____

_____

_____

_____

_____

_____

_____

_____

Keep trying to offer yourself as much compassion and grace as you can that you often should all over yourself when your healthy wants and desires go unmet. Life is difficult and painful for many reasons, but one of the main reasons is that we or others get in the way of getting the healthy things we want in life.

Chris Thurman, Ph.D.

I want to pat you on the back for reading this book and completing the workbook. I hope both were helpful to you. I will be praying for you that you will increasingly break free from the shoulds and shouldn'ts you have in life, and that you will no longer should all over yourself. Please have compassion and grace for just how difficult it is being an imperfect person in a world full of imperfect people like yourself. Bathe everything in as much empathy and kindness as you can.

Best wishes as you make the journey from condemnation to compassion.

Appendix A

Recommended Reading That Will Help You Stop Shoulding All Over Yourself

Addiction
Addiction and Grace by Gerald May
Addictions: A Banquet in the Grave by Ed Welch

Anger
The Anger Workbook by Les Carter and Frank Minirth

Anxiety/Worry
Calm My Anxious Heart by Linda Dillow
The Anxiety Cure by Archibald Hart
The Worry Workbook by Les Carter and Frank Minirth

Balance
In Search of Balance by Richard Swenson
Margin by Richard Swenson

Bonding/Attachments
Hold Me Tight by Sue Johnson
How We Love by Milan and Kay Yerkovich
Wired for Love by Stan Tatkin and Harville Hendrix

Boundaries/Peacemaking
Boundaries by Henry Cloud and John Townsend
The Peacemaker by Ken Sande

Depression
Happiness is a Choice by Frank Minirth and Paul Meier
The Depression Cure by Stephen Ilardi
The Mindful Way Through Depression by Mark Williams,
　　　John Teasdale, Zindel Segal, and Jon Kabat-Zinn

Emotional/Spiritual Health
Changes that Heal by Henry Cloud
Emotionally Healthy Spirituality by Peter Scazzero
Renovation of the Heart by Dallas Willard
The Divine Conspiracy by Dallas Willard
The Road Less Traveled by Scott Peck

Forgiveness
Five Steps to Forgiveness by Everett Worthington
The Art of Forgiving by Lewis Smedes
Total Forgiveness by R.T. Kendall

God
Knowing God by J. I. Packer
Knowledge of the Holy by A. W. Tozer

Grace
Grace Awakening by Charles Swindoll
What's So Amazing about Grace? by Phillip Yancey

Marriage
Boundaries in Marriage by Henry Cloud and John Town-
　　　send
Hope for the Separated by Gary Chapman
Sacred Marriage by Gary Thomas
Saving Your Marriage Before It Starts by Les and Leslie Par-
　　　rott
The Five Love Languages by Gary Chapman
The Lies Couples Believe by Chris Thurman
The Meaning of Marriage by Tim and Kathy Keller
The Mystery of Marriage by Mike Mason

Men's Issues
I Don't Want to Talk about It by Terence Real
Men in Mid-Life Crisis by Jim Conway
Men's Secret Wars by Patrick Means
Point Man by Steve Farrar
The Man in the Mirror by Patrick Worley
When Men Think Private Thoughts by Gordon MacDonald
Wild at Heart by John Eldredge

Mindfulness
10% Happier: How I Tamed the Voice in My Head, Reduced Stress Without Losing My Edge and Found Self-Help that Actually Works—A True Story by Dan Harris
Mindfulness: An Eight-Week Plan for Finding Peace in a Frantic World by Mark Williams and Danny Penman
Mindfulness and Christian Spirituality: Making Space for God by Tim Stead
Mindsight: The New Science of Personal Transformation by Daniel Siegel
Right Here Right Now: The Practice of Christian Mindfulness by Amy Oden
The Untethered Soul: The Journey Beyond Yourself by Michael A. Singer
Wherever You Go There You Are: Mindfulness Meditation in Everyday Life by Jon Kabat-Zinn

Personality Disorders
Freeing Yourself from the Narcissists in Your Life by Linda Martinez-Lewi
Stop Walking on Eggshells by Paul Mason and Randi Kreger
The Sociopath Next Door by Martha Stout
Why Is It Always About You? by Sandy Hotchkiss

Renewing Your Mind

Feeling Good by David Burns

Get Out of Your Head by Jennie Allen

Get Out of Your Mind and Into Your Life by Stephen Hayes

Mind Over Mood by Dennis Greenberger and Christine Padesky

Telling Yourself the Truth by William Backus and Marie Chapian

The Lies We Believe by Chris Thurman

The Lies We Believe About God by Chris Thurman

Self-Compassion

Self-Compassion: Stop Beating Yourself Up and Leave Insecurity Behind by Kristin Neff

The Mindful Self-Compassion Book: A Proven Way to Accept Yourself, Build Inner Strength, and Thrive by Kristin Neff and Christopher Germer

The Self-Compassion Skills Workbook: A 14-Day Plan to Transform Your Relationship with Yourself by Tim Desmond

Shame

Healing the Shame that Binds You by John Bradshaw

I Thought It Was Just Me by Brene Brown

Shame Interrupted by Ed Welch

The Gifts of Imperfection by Brene Brown

The Soul of Shame by Curt Thompson

Suffering

Disappointment with God by Phillip Yancey

Where is God When it Hurts? by Phillip Yancey

Women's Issues

Breaking Free by Beth Moore

Ever After by Vicki Courtney

Finding Peace for Your Heart by Stormie Omartian

Healing the Soul of a Woman by Joyce Meyer

Lord, I Want to be Whole by Stormie Omartian
Rest Assured by Vicki Courtney
So Long, Insecurity by Beth Moore

Worth
The Search for Significance by Robert McGee

Appendix B

References

All the quotations in the book, are from A-Z Quotes
https://www.azquotes.com/

Appendix C

Favorite 'Should' Quotations

Let go of who you think you should be in order to be who you are. Be imperfect and have compassion for yourself.
--Brene Brown

Should is a futile word. It's about what didn't happen. It belongs in a parallel universe. It belongs in another dimension of space.
--Margaret Atwood

"Should be" will always be a long road.
--S. Kelly Harrell

Strike the word should from your vocabulary.
--Scott Mautz

There is no way you should feel, there is only the way you feel.
--Akiroq Brost

He should be the utmost of honesty, generosity, considerateness, justice, dignity, courage, unselfishness. He should be the perfect lover, husband, teacher. He should be able to endure everything, should like everybody, should love his parents, his wife, his country; or he should not be attached to anything or anybody, nothing should matter to him, he should never feel hurt, and he should always be serene and unruffled. He should always enjoy life; or he should be above pleasure and enjoyment. He should be spontaneous; he should al-

ways control his feelings. He should know, understand, and foresee everything. He should be able to solve every problem of his own, or of others, in no time. He should be able to overcome every difficulty of his as soon as he sees it. He should never be tired or fall ill. He should always be able to find a job. He should be able to do in one hour which can only be done in two to three hours.
—Karen Horney

Women most often experience shame as a web of layered, conflicting, and competing social-community expectations. The expectations dictate who we should be, what we should be, how we should be.
--Brene Brown

… don't worry too much about what someone else says you 'should' do. Know what you want to do and why it's important to you.
--Melissa Steginus

'Shoulds' come only from leftover thinking. If we are truly in this moment (the only one there really is), we don't should on ourselves.
--Kelly Corbet

Should is my all time least favorite word. It's this sort of guilt inducing, finger wagging word that we use to beat up others and ourselves.
--Frank Beddor

The creative person has to dissolve all shoulds and should nots.
--Osho

No good sentences ever include the word 'should.'
--Cassandra Clare

So where does all this "shoulding" leave us? For many the answer is depressed and anxious. For millions it leads to taking meds to control their anxiety instead of changing the thinking patterns that cause the anxiety in the first place. So many people "should" on themselves regularly with high, unrealistic expectations. They are very driven, perfectionistic, achievement-oriented and outer goal-focused. I call this being a human doing rather than a human being.
--Andrea Wachter

Don't 'should' on yourself, instead, replace it with 'could' and add an alternative option.
--Amber Khan

As a culture, we are often held captive by the internalized voice of what we think we're supposed to do and be. We use the word should so frequently that it takes the place of more accurate and powerful phrases like *"I want," "I can," and "I will."* As a culture, we are often held captive by the internalized voice of what we think we're supposed to do and be. We use the word should so frequently that it takes the place of more accurate and powerful phrases like *"I want," "I can," and "I will."*
--Jesse Kneeland

There's a word that I decided to drop from my vocabulary. It's the word *should*. It comes from the word *shall*, which in Old English means "to be under an obligation" or "to owe." *Should* often represents something I've obligated myself to do—without even realizing it. The *shoulds* are the belief systems I unwittingly adopted. The *shoulds* are the expectations of other people about how I'm supposed to live my life. The *shoulds* are my own prison, the iron bars that constrain my thinking, and the chains that hold me back.
--Ozan Varol

255

For many of us, we have lived in a "should world" our whole lives. Our parents, our teachers, our Sunday school lessons and our peers have showered us with shoulds since we were old enough to remember. Sure, they are meant to be used as a "guide" and to mold our character into a moral being but sometimes they go a little too far. They step beyond the boundaries of character building and making wise decisions and begin an ongoing inner dialogue of shaming ourselves into something that we may not be.
--Kelly, The Invisible Warrior

Change the should into a request or a preference. Instead of angrily saying, "You should have introduced me to your cousin!" you can say, "I wish you had introduced me to your cousin." Instead of insisting, "You must not smoke in the house!" you can say, "I'd prefer that you smoke outside."
--Clifford Lazarus

And really, *should* is most often a result of comparison. I *should* be thinner, sexier, less talkative, more thoughtful, a better parent, you insert the adjective. Today I am judging myself based on my productivity about how I am using my hours. In a split second I created an unreasonable standard for myself that became an instant joy-sucker.
--Shelly Miller

Everyone's internal dialogue plays a major role in their daily lives... including the formation of goals. Here's the problem. If your internal dialogue uses the word 'should'... you probably are either setting no goals at all, or some, many or all the ones you do set will never be achieved.
--Jon Sooy

ABOUT
KHARIS PUBLISHING

KHARIS PUBLISHING is an independent, traditional publishing house with a core mission to publish impactful books, and channel proceeds into establishing mini-libraries or resource centers for orphanages in developing countries, so these kids will learn to read, dream, and grow. Every time you purchase a book from Kharis Publishing or partner as an author, you are helping give these kids an amazing opportunity to read, dream, and grow. Kharis Publishing is an imprint of Kharis Media LLC. Learn more at;
https://www.kharispublishing.com

Printed in the USA
CPSIA information can be obtained
at www.ICGtesting.com
LVHW011435150724
785516LV00023B/412